AN ADMIRABLE FACULTY

Recruiting, Hiring, Training, and Retaining the Best Independent School Teachers

by

Peter Gow

One Schoolhouse
1342 Florida Avenue NW
Washington, DC 20009

LICENSING AND COPYRIGHT

2020

.epub ISBN: 978-1-7342479-8-5
.pdf ISBN: 978-1-7342479-9-2
.mobi ISBN: 978-1-7346348-0-8
Paperback ISBN: 978-1-7346348-1-5

ABOUT THE AUTHOR

Peter Gow has been a teacher and an administrator in independent schools for over 40 years. He grew up on the campus of The Gow School and graduated from Nichols School in Buffalo, New York, before attending college at Yale and graduate school at Brown. He taught at The Gow School, Providence Country Day School, The Fessenden School, and Beaver Country Day School. He was a founding board member and then executive director of the Independent Curriculum Group and joined One Schoolhouse as Independent Curriculum Resource Director when the ICG merged with One Schoolhouse in 2019. Peter has written, consulted, and presented for schools and national educational organizations in the United States and Canada.

Table of Contents

To my late spouse,
Mimi Harrington,
and to my late father,
David Whitcomb Gow,
admirable teachers both!

Foreword
(from the 2005 National Association
of Independent Schools edition)

For nearly a hundred years now members of my family have started each fall as members of the faculty—and often the administration—of independent schools. For my grandfather, who began at Choate in the fall of 1906, entry into the teaching fraternity was an act of social mobility, the next logical step upward from the tenements of a factory town after a scholarship-funded college career. Having attended Yale with the sons of gentlemen, he would now teach them, transmuting his love of Classical languages and English literature—still a suspect field in those days— into a respectable if modest living. I don't know whether he had planned on making it a career, but a teacher he remained until his death. Even as headmaster of the school he founded, he continued to teach a full load of classes and to read deeply in the professional literature of his particular field of interest, the education of dyslexic students.

In time my grandfather fathered six children, the youngest of whom made the transition from graduate school into teaching, from which he retired (as a head of school) in 1990. Like my father, I too entered the profession as a stopgap after graduate school and found myself captivated. About a third of my 20-some cousins and siblings have taught at some point in their lives, and the next generation already has its own share of teachers.

When I share this story with other teachers, I soon learn how many of us come from tribes of educators. Commenting on the lack of remuneration and prestige associated with teaching, someone inevitably makes a joke about "bad genes," and we dutifully smile. When we associate with people who work in the "business world"—often acquaintances with whom we share an educational background but distinctly *not* an income level—we may feel a bit abashed and sometimes even downright ashamed. Inevitably, there is at least one disapproving voice ready to comment on those "summers off," supposedly indicative of teachers' lassitude and unwillingness to take on the harsh realities of the workaday world. We are either patronized as holy innocents or gently condemned as so hopelessly naïve that we cannot even look out for own interests. Sadly, it is not uncommon for us to make or introduce these assumptions ourselves, internal oppression that only adds to the estrangement that teachers often feel from "mainstream" workers.

But I don't believe it is a genetic malady or a spectacular inability to take care of ourselves that characterizes those of us who choose to teach. The work of teaching, above all, represents a set of complex relationships— among adults, students, and institutions. The decision to enter and remain in teaching represents conscious sacrifices made as we embrace that complexity. To become a teacher is to perform an act of faith. To remain in the profession is a sustained act of humanity. For some, it is a true vocation, a priesthood, while for others it simply involves doing deeply satisfying work in an emotionally congenial setting. Many of us find it a lifelong calling; for others it is a byway—sometimes an influence on life to come, sometimes not—along a winding career path. Whatever we call it does not so much matter when we are doing it and finding it meaningful.

In this book, I explore the sources and meanings of that enjoyment, those relationships, and those values, focusing specifically on the world of North American independent schools. In my subtitle—recruiting, hiring, training, retaining, and retiring—is encoded my life's work and that of my peers. How is the relationship between teacher and school forged? How is it maintained in a mutually beneficial manner—for better and for worse— and how can it be brought to a graceful point of separation that allows both partners to go on living and growing? When the course of the relationship runs smooth, the benefit to all parties can be inestimable and its effects both profound and beautiful.

At the risk of sounding simplistic, the approach I take in this book is to reduce the life cycle of a teaching career, from the first notice of an opening until the teacher's retirement, to a dozen maxims. Each presents an essential, irreducible truth; one has several corollaries. A few are likely to be controversial, as they gainsay truths that some educators hold dear.

I imagine, though, that anyone reading this is already at least a little bit open to new ideas; if your school is already perfect or your hiring instinct has proven infallible (so far), you don't need this book, anyhow. But if you are thinking hard about what recent National Association of Independent Schools research has rated the second most challenging issue facing independent schools today, after making independent schooling affordable, you are probably looking for guidance. Don't let the brevity of my maxims fool you, and do not be tempted to read what follows as a "cookbook" from which you may choose the ideas that seem congenial and reject or ignore those that seem too complex or that are antithetical to your current views or practices. Picking and choosing here would be possible, but the overall point of this volume is to invite schools to take what might be called a systems approach the whole matter of hiring and retention.

As you will discover, I believe firmly that good teachers are not just born; they can be made. It is the responsibility of all schools to make the very best teachers they can, and schools must account this work as second in importance only to reaching each student—a goal from which making good teachers cannot really be separated.

The Twelve Maxims on which this book is based are little mantras. If practiced, I believe they can help a school become the kind of community in which the nurturing of teachers from raw recruits into seasoned, effective, and even beloved professionals becomes the norm. Such a school will have no trouble enacting its mission and its culture will be so welcoming and engaging on all levels that it will have little trouble attracting either students or faculty.

This claim may seem grandiose, but I hope readers will find that the overall approach of this book fully acknowledges and embraces the complexities of describing good teaching and prescribing how to achieve it. Teaching has never been an easy thing to talk or write about, because so much of teaching is about the heart. Schools, being communities of the head and heart both, are even harder to capture in words. To analyze the relationships between teachers and schools is more difficult still.

What follows is a book of practical suggestions about the role of the school in building and sustaining those relationships, a "how-to" manual that hopes to acknowledge the primacy of the heart and soul of its users. The suggestions made are many, and a number of them are expensive in terms of money, time, or both. It is unlikely that any "model school" will either choose to or be able to implement all of them, and there are some with which the reader may flatly disagree. All schools must accommodate themselves to limitations on resources as well as to their attachment to existing practice. That is as it should be, or at least as it must be.

There is another not-so-hidden agenda to this book: the desire to expand the ways in which independent education thinks of and treats itself as a true profession. One aspect of this involves the open sharing of ideas and practices among schools. Too often schools, particularly those with a long record of success, regard themselves as having little to learn from other educators or other schools. This attitude would be fatal in medicine or law, where the exchange of information and new knowledge has been the basis for all progress. The efforts of the National Association of Independent Schools (hereafter referred to only as NAIS), regional associations, the editors of the new Independent Teacher on-line journal, and several listservs devoted to independent school concerns represent significant progress in this area, and I hope that this book will add something to the field.

Another aspect of professionalism in independent school teaching has to do with the expectations we have for teachers. Thankfully, the days are gone when "professional development" was something that "real" teachers avoided like the plague, but the idea that teachers must be engaged in a lifelong process of keeping up in their field—not simply their subject area but the entire realm of child development, pedagogy, curriculum, and assessment—is still in its infancy in many places. I would go so far as to argue that independent school people, for the most part liberated from government mandates that seem bent on reducing public education to standardized testing and regulatory compliance, are blessed with the freedom to pursue the knowledge of education in its essence. That freedom bears with it a responsibility for independent schools to recruit, train, evaluate, reward, and generally maintain their faculties as respected communities of true professionals. The stakes, after all, are enormous: our children and our future.

Peter Gow
Dedham, Massachusetts

Addendum and a note on the text for the 2020 One Schoolhouse edition

It may be naivete, hubris, or the onset of dementia, but I believe that much of what I wrote sixteen years ago still stands. That said, I have worked through the text here to update what needs updating, and in the Age of Google I have eliminated the retrospectively meager "Resource" sections that accompanied each chapter; a quick search here and there can supply many more useful ideas than could be found in the original. (I have also linked a few sites, which e-book readers can access handily, as well.)

Some years after the publication of An Admirable Faculty I was seized again by the writing bug and wrote what is in my mind a kind of companion volume to this: The Intentional Teacher: Forging a Great Career in the Independent School Classroom. Intentional is still in print and available from its publisher, Avocus, and it lays out many of the same issues found here from the teacher's-eye view rather than the "school's-eye" view presented here.

Textual considerations: As a past foster "parent" very conscious of how the child differentiated us from his biological family, I have tried to avoid the use of the term "parent" in this edition, replacing it with parent/guardian or the more serviceable "family." I believe schools should all make a point of considering this language in all their communications. Lately I heard about a school that changed the name of their Parent Association to "Family Association"—bravo!

I subscribe to the use of gender-free general pronouns, including the singular "they" and "themself." These are real things these days, even if old Grammar Police may be stroking their nightsticks in consternation. But be prepared.

Please enjoy and hopefully find practical value in *An Admirable Faculty*, 2020 edition. It is still my truth.

> Peter Gow
> (still writing in the
> same chair in Dedham,
> Massachusetts)

Chapter One
Preparation for Hiring

Maxim One: Every opening is an opportunity.

Anyone who has ever worked in a school has felt that sharp pang of impending loss upon hearing of a colleague's decision to leave. If the colleague has been even vaguely competent and sociable, this pang resonates throughout the entire school—students, staff, and families. "What will we do without Mr. So-and-so?" we ask. "How can we possibly replace him?" Often our questions proceed to the very specific: "What about the tennis team, or the Model U.N.?" Sometimes we take the matter personally: "How could he leave me here?"

We truly mourn at some of these announcements, for the students, for the institution, for ourselves. We experience the anguish of separation and the stages of grief. Sometimes the feelings unleashed by the prospect of separation are surprising. Some of us may envy a person we see as moving on to a new, happier—and often more remunerative—stage of life or escaping an unhappy community. Others may feel angry with the leaver for

1

letting us down or for letting down the institution or the students. Many of us will simply miss a friend, a familiar face in the faculty room or the dining hall.

As we shall see later on, when a long-term faculty or community member retires, a school's administration should carefully manage the event. But for any departure, the administration faces a specific and concrete issue: filling the position being vacated.

As much as possible, it will behoove the administration to cast as unemotional an eye as possible on the situation. A position is open. A new person, or perhaps new persons, must be hired. Jobs must be done: teaching, coaching, advising, running a dormitory or an activity. And perhaps there are also important but not formally acknowledged roles to be filled: faculty meeting gadfly, dining room wag, unofficial sheriff of the bleachers at home games. However much the leave-taking may distress the school, all of these open jobs and open roles must be viewed as opportunities.

Each school maintains a set of aspirations, goals, and needs. Some, like the mission or the published goals of a strategic plan, are explicit, while many more are unstated or even something of a secret. They may relate to programs—"We need to be more like Such-and-such School," or "have more AP Scholars" or "win more swim meets"—or they may relate to the nature of the school community—"We need to attract more students from this or that neighborhood or feeder school" or "have more families and faculty of color." The concerns may even be much more materialistic—"We must get that million-dollar gift from the Smiths!" Any ten people in your school could make a list of these goals and aspirations, and in a secure and open community it is likely that everyone's lists would coincide pretty well.

The impending departure of a member of the faculty is above all a chance for the school to take specific steps toward achieving some of those aspirations. This is the moment when someone, or some small group of people specifically charged with doing so, should be taking stock of the school's needs and thinking about how filling the vacant position can help meet some of those needs. This is not being hard-hearted, but merely practical. A school that despairs of filling Mr. So-and-So's shoes before the search has even begun is sacrificing an opportunity.

The fact is, Mr. So-and-So's shoes cannot be filled and there is little point in trying to do so. The point is not to fill his shoes but rather to figure out where Mr. So-and-So stands and then to see how the next person, or the next configuration of people standing in the same spot, can move the school forward in specific ways. Mr. So-and-So may have been a towering giant, but there are other giants out there, and other ways to achieve great stature. Even as a beloved giant, Mr. So-and-So may have been a problematic presence in some areas. A flood of new ideas or initiatives may be released as he makes his way down the driveway. The school must recognize and anticipate all these factors and conditions.

Along with the opportunities for future progress that a faculty departure may offer, there are equally valuable possibilities for institutional self-examination and reflection. Some of these are of modest worth; others can be enormously helpful in planning for the school's future.

When a departure is announced, the next question is, "Why? Where are they going?" Data collected by Jim Pugh at the Brooks School (Massachusetts) and several of his colleagues around the Northeast in the early 2000s showed that most independent school teachers leave positions for "personal reasons," and that many go on to other teaching jobs in independent schools. Over the years, Pugh and his colleagues have learned, school turnover nationally ranges somewhere in the area of 8 to 10 percent. Younger teachers tend to return to graduate school or to begin families. Boarding school teachers tend to move toward day schools. Pugh's figures do not specify a figure for teachers not being rehired, and it is difficult to tease from his data a sense of the number of teachers who are "going away mad," but the sense of the data is that people leave teaching jobs for good and positive reasons.

But in the case of an individual departure from a single school, who is leaving and why matter a great deal. Sometimes the reasons are negative. A teacher may not have been asked back due to some aspect of professional performance, and there are teachers—even great ones, I would maintain—for whom a particular school is not a good match. And some people just grow weary and testy and know themselves well enough—even if they cast blame elsewhere—to realize it is time to move on.

More often, as Pugh's data reassures us, the reasons are based on personal needs that simply cannot be met by employment at the school. A lonely but professionally happy teacher may wish just to move on to a larger community or to be nearer to friends and family. Some may decide that teaching isn't the career they want, so a job change or new training is in order. These are the "time of life" changes. A young family person may hope to make a decisive career move, or an older one may wish to move to a community closer to the site of a planned retirement down the road.

Marriage or partnership, the need to care for aging parents, the desire to spend more time with children—all of these are unexceptionable reasons for teachers to leave schools and most have little or nothing to do with the school itself. They are, at least on the face of it, the unavoidable, "no-fault" attrition that all schools experience.

Nonetheless, schools should monitor the reasons for faculty departures and, despite the small size of the sample, make some comparisons over time both to national trends and to the school's sense of itself. Are our families feeling valued on campus? Are there opportunities here for young and mid-career teachers to keep growing? Do the school and the surrounding community provide enough social stimulation for single faculty or faculty of color? Is the school an incubator for educators or just a way station on the road to law or business school? Do senior faculty really feel valued?

Great consternation can arise in a school community when there is a perception that faculty turnover is unwholesomely high. Even when the departures are all attributable to "time of life" reasons, a percentage change outside the norm—in excess, say, of 15 to 20 percent—or the loss of one or two highly visible people will start tongues wagging and heads shaking. Most schools have experienced years when a confluence of personal factors has meant a frenzy of hiring and a season spent defending the school's honor in conversations about faculty turnover.

When some of the leavers are in fact going away angry, and especially if they are being vocal about it, even a few departures can feel like an exodus. Such a situation should be cause for self-examination. And in those rare and terrible situations in which a mass migration actually is taking place, failure to delve into its causes represents not just lost opportunity but a serious failure of both leadership and stewardship.

It may be heretical to do so, but it is worth wondering out loud whether a school with unnaturally low faculty attrition over a period of years may have its own problems. The school may be the Elysian Fields for faculty, but is it a place where innovation, individual growth, and the kind of dynamism that drives great schools can be found? Or is the school enabling a culture of status quo that is moribund or mediocre? How, when the inevitable time of change comes, will the community welcome and adapt to the presence of newcomers and new ideas?

No matter why people are going, at the end of each school year, a school should gather data for ongoing study of its own staffing issues. The simplest way to do this, other than recording in some form other than memory lore the names of departing faculty, is to conduct exit interviews with everyone who is leaving. Ideally, these should be conducted by someone outside the academic administrative structure (at my own school, this has been done by the director of admission), and certainly by someone without an evaluative role. A school might even consider hiring an outside consultant; there are specialists in employment issues who do this routinely.

The exit interviews themselves should focus on questions relating to employee quality of life. What did the teacher find satisfying or rewarding about working at the school? Did the teacher feel supported in the community? Have there been special factors of a positive or negative nature in the teacher's experience? Interviews should not be fishing expeditions aimed at uncovering confirmation of previously identified issues, but if there are known areas of concern, the interviews should not avoid them. The point of the interview is to capture a snapshot of life at the school and to compile a composite picture of the things that have both pleased and displeased the people who are leaving. Through this process, the disinterested interviewer who can promise anonymity can gather information that van be extraordinarily useful in making the school a better place to live, work, and learn.

Even if exit interviews are conducted too late to have an effect on the current hiring season, the results—stripped of any personal attribution—should be reviewed by the administration at the highest appropriate level and then passed on to the school's Hiring Team (see Chapter Two). While some data may be disregarded or taken with a grain of salt, patterns, and in particular patterns that recur from year to year, should be noted. Positive things can be recognized, strengthened, or made explicit. Negative factors may need appropriate attention; sometimes the knowledge that teachers are leaving for a particular reason may be just the evidence needed to spur action. Exit interview data can either quash or confirm a vague sense, rumor, or intuition, and do so in a concrete way.

The leave-taking of a faculty member or the departure of a group of respected teachers can be sad and even troubling, but these events also can give a school a reason and an opening to do some necessary and valuable self-examination. Schools that see this work not as a chore but as an opportunity will find themselves increasingly successful in attracting and hiring good candidates.

Best Practices
in Preparation For Hiring

- Consider each position opening a significant opportunity for school improvement.

- Be aware of all the school's broadest needs and goals in terms of: strategic direction; curriculum and pedagogy; non-academic program improvement; institutional advancement and enrollment management.

- Track the reasons for faculty departures over time. Which are "no-fault" attrition or "time of life" departures, and who is leaving because they are simply looking for a more congenial work environment? Look for trends and patterns.

- Conduct anonymous, open-ended exit interviews with all departing employees; consider engaging consulting help in this area.

- Review departure tracking and exit interview data at the administrative level annually. Address worrisome trends and patterns.

Chapter Two
Building the Recruiting Case

Maxim Two: Know thyself.

Each year independent schools in North America fill something on the order of thousands of teaching positions. While this figure is a small drop in the bucket of the total employment picture, it represents a highly specialized and highly committed workforce. With independent school teacher turnover estimated at being close to ten percent, recruiting new faculty is an annual fact of life in schools. Identifying potential candidates, evaluating them based on qualifications and the potential for "match," and enticing them into the school community is time-consuming, but, if done thoroughly and thoughtfully, it is work with enormous payoff. Simply conducting a series of narrowly focused departmental recruiting efforts or culling the résumé pile for plausible "triple threats" (teaching, coaching, dorm supervision) may cause the school to miss out on making substantial improvements in programs not directly associated with the searches.

Independent schools are as different one from another as snowflakes. Most schools are fairly clear with themselves as to what distinguishes their programs and community, and the admission office probably has a pretty effective spiel about the school's unique qualities. Using this information to attract new members of the school's professional community ought to be regarded as even more important than recruiting students. Each teacher and each coach bears responsibility for carrying out some aspect of the school's mission. Each represents the school to parents, to the local community, to other educators, and, most importantly, to students, for whom every faculty member is in some way a living embodiment of the school's values and beliefs. Grouchy or slipshod teaching, apathetic coaching, and careless supervision send messages to all students about what really matters at the school. These powerful messages, unfortunately, can easily offset the positive and inspiring lessons learned in great classes or at moving community events.

By closely considering three areas—the nature of the school and its community, the needs of the school, and the school's "cultural geography"—you can become more intentional and successful in using the recruiting process to build a faculty of capable educators committed to the institution and the community—and who are ready to stay there for a while.

As any self-help magazine quiz will tell you, the way to make yourself attractive to others is to be confident in who you are. This should be a compelling truth for a school, as well. An independent school's mission and nature are the essential ingredients of successful faculty recruiting, and while the one can be written down in a neatly turned paragraph or two, the other needs to be evaluated, clarified, and articulated on a regular basis in order for a school truly to "know itself." Only then can the school confidently assess its staffing needs and consider the best way to find and ultimately hire candidates who will be a good match—for the school as it is, and as it aspires to be.

Creating this match requires self-assessment. Certain obvious philosophical or structural factors—religious affiliation, grade levels taught, progressive mission, strong "family" structure, farm-based, experiential, boarding or day, with housing or without—are central to recruiting faculty. But cultural factors of many sorts are also important and, in the end, determining. How formal is the school? To what degree are its policies driven by tradition or by external expectations? How successful has the school been (or how successful does it want to be) in creating a multicultural community of faculty and students? To what extent do real-world politics matter—is the school a bastion of Republican virtue, or does

13

the community lean to the left? In either case, how comfortable are dissenters made to feel? And of course, how are the pay and benefits?

A thoughtful and successful faculty recruitment program will take into account the question, "What sort of school are we?" First and foremost, faculty recruiting, like strategic planning, fund raising, and student recruiting, must be built around the school's mission. This should go without saying, but to make explicit the relationship between a school's mission and values and the nature and lives of its faculty and staff is a healthy act of reflection that should be ongoing—certainly occurring more frequently than once every 10 years as part of an accreditation self-study. Furthermore, the exercise will be even more valuable if, instead of concentrating on perceived needs for the future, the analysis includes a close look at what sorts of people are already thriving in the school's environment.

Who should perform this exercise? Ideally, the formation of a Hiring Team should be the earliest task in the recruiting and hiring cycle. In a large school, this work may be divided up by division, but the team should include key administrators who supervise teachers. Depending on the school's values and goals, the team could include, along with the division director, academic dean or dean of faculty, and, *ex officio*, the head of school, the person in charge of athletics or extracurricular activities, the chief diversity officer, the director of residential life, the director of the advisory system, and perhaps a classroom teacher and/or, in a school whose mission and culture are avowedly student-centered, a student. Team members should be responsible for interviewing candidates and, with the department chair or program director with whom the new person will be working most directly, making the final recommendation or decision to offer a position.

In a perfect world, the Hiring Team should be privy to the results of exit interviews and to any discussions about policies or practices that have resulted from them. The team's knowledge of specific issues related to the school's work environment could inform future decisions.

The Hiring Team should be formed well before the actual hiring season begins. Along with an identification of known and anticipated needs, the team should have a brief but thoughtful discussion of the following questions about important aspects of the school's mission and culture as experienced and shaped by teachers:

- What are the key values of the school, as stated in the mission and in other public documents?

- What does the school most want to accomplish in the next five to 10 years?

- In a single phrase, what is the essential task of teachers at the school?
- What is the "glue" that holds the school community together—the academic curriculum, dormitory life, shared values or faith, athletics or performances, a particular ritual or tradition?
- Where does the school community's "center of gravity" lie—with students, faculty, administrators, parents, an external body?
- What is unique about the school? How or where would a prospective teacher see or experience this specialness?
- What are the most important attributes of the kind of person who will be able to carry out the mission?
- What is asked of a faculty member at the school?
- What are the special rewards of teaching at the school?
- What are the special challenges of teaching at the school?
- Does the school culture truly support and value people who bring or raise new ideas?

- What are some common characteristics of people who have thrived and grown in this school community?

- What are some common characteristics of people who have not been a good match for the school?

It may seem a waste of time to have conversations about these topics, on which there may be general agreement and where the answers may be obvious to all. Nevertheless, to address each of these questions explicitly is to ensure that members of the team are all "on the same page" and that problematic areas are identified. The conversation around each question need not be exhaustive, but it should address the salient issues. Team members should develop a picture of the essential qualities of the school community and of the sort of person likely to fit in well and be a real contributor. This will be useful in planning how to recruit and cultivate pools of appropriate candidates for specific openings and in developing a clear sense of which candidates will be likely to make the best *long-term* matches for the school

Spending some time talking about questions like these will also pay off during the actual interviewing and hiring process, through the development of common responses to important questions as well as some shared language for talking about the school. If the talking points developed by the Hiring Team grow out of serious and honest reflection, they will ring true to applicants and be consistent in message if not wording; one thing that re-assures interviewees is hearing a sincere and consistent message from a prospective school. (Obviously, "pat" answers that sound more like a party line than the real story are to be avoided.)

The Hiring Team should also spend some time discussing the broad needs of the school and the opportunities that open positions may present. Each person who joins the staff of an independent school should represent a rock-solid response to the immediate needs of the position, whether the hire is an experienced teacher of Asian history, a reliable junior varsity hockey coach, a newspaper advisor, or an expert in early childhood education. The new hire should also bring a level of "added value" that truly might make the institution better.

The idea of "value added" makes the new hire an opportunity for the school. The entire hiring process should be devoted to moving the school a step closer to clearly understood goals: a department more knowledgeable in a particular area; a solid sub-varsity athletic program; a significantly better student news-paper; a pre-kindergarten that can grow. While this would seem self-evident, it is important for the school to have a master plan of its larger needs as it approaches the hiring season. The Hiring Team should either make the plan itself or be given a direct mandate from a higher authority.

The hiring season might typically begin with a meeting of the administrators involved in the recruiting and hiring process: the head of school; the division heads; the chief diversity officer; the dean of students (or whoever oversees the afternoon program and the athletic department); the director of residential life (if boarding); and the academic dean. They begin with a quick review of the school's annual goals in certain broad areas (academic program, school life, advancement) based on the institutional strategic plan as well as a general conversation around other institutional needs. The group may also brainstorm a list of basic desiderata: Wouldn't it be great to have a debate team, or more males in the middle school, or a charismatic instructor to move the dance program forward? At this point, few or possibly none of the school's specific hiring needs may be clear, but the group is able to devote the meeting to identifying interesting ways in which new human resources might be used.

At this point the Hiring Team should develop a rough list of institutional needs, which need not be confined to specific aspects of job descriptions. Other qualities that school may be seeking more of—youth, humor, married couples, gravitas, diversity of a specific sort, intellectualism—should be included in this list, making special note of those qualities that have been identified as related to success in the school community. Although in a month or two there may be an urgent need to find a subject specialist or a highly skilled coach in a particular sport, the first pass in the Hiring Team's needs review ought to be made from an institutional perspective. From this discussion comes an informal "wish list" for the year. Focus on fundamental questions, such as:

1. What does the school community need overall, in terms of:
   - pedagogical expertise
   - content-area expertise
   - student service outside the classroom
   - athletic or extracurricular expertise
   - faculty leadership
   - gender, age, or cultural balance or diversity?

2. What are some other areas of program and culture that could use some development in ways that "new blood" might make possible?

3. What interesting ideas have surfaced that might be helped along by some new expertise or enthusiasm?

The school ALSO needs to come to a clear understanding of certain geographical factors. You cannot do much about whether your location is urban or rural, Midwestern or on the East Coast, but you can take stock of what your location, community size, and physical environment mean to those who teach at your school and those who might apply. While this issue relates very much to school culture in its broadest sense when it comes to retention, at the recruiting stage a strategic institution will make sure that it has gathered pertinent data that can be made available to teaching candidates in the form of well-grounded answers and information, not just optimistic or reassuring platitudes. In this area above all, a school must both keep the conversation real and demonstrate its willingness to work with a candidate in processing geographical issues.

When searching recently for some information about a large boarding school in a rural area, I found several websites for on-line dating services listed at the school address. These services represented, I realized, the efforts of young, single faculty to meet peers. As anyone who has been a single faculty member in such a place knows, the opportunities for making new social contacts are few. I wondered if the school actively supported the dating games being played by its young teachers. If so, it might be a positive and thoughtful response on the part of the school to a real need of its faculty—a response that could play a significant role in teacher retention.

Geographical factors can be very much at play in the area of diversity. Few individuals will elect to be the only member of a particular minority group within a 50-mile radius unless they are assured that the school is committed to making sure that its faculty and students of color have ample opportunity to engage with their communities—through active membership in regional diversity organizations, through attendance at NAIS's annual People of Color Conference, or through the school's own commitment to diversity and multiculturalism. Even a school that is geographically removed from racial diversity or whose members are primarily white can work at being a community in which multiculturalism is alive and well (see Chapter Three). Schools at the early stages of building faculty diversity would be well served by giving thought up front—even to the extent of engaging outside expertise—to how a monocultural environment can be made welcoming to new kinds of members.

Size, region, and setting are issues about which some schools become painfully aware as they struggle with finding faculty willing to relocate to a remote area or to settle in a city with stratospheric housing costs. For boarding schools housing may not be an issue, and even some day schools in expensive communities have moved to provide some below-market rentals for faculty. In some areas the reverse is true and boarding schools have a difficult time keeping faculty on campus when local housing costs are low; schools respond by providing better housing and in some cases by offering stipends to dormitory faculty. Other pay and benefit schemes, such as helping younger faculty pay down student loans, can also be used to target particular candidate demographics.

Schools with unique philosophical or strong religious foundations or other unusual situations (besides deep pockets) must be especially self-aware in developing their recruiting strategies. While it may be obvious that an atheist might be an unlikely candidate for a position in a strongly faith-based school, it might be less clear that a recent graduate of a highly competitive university, a heavy hitter by conventional educational standards, might have a hard time adjusting to the ways of a non-traditional or progressive environment even if they may be intellectually intrigued by the approach. Single-sex schools have long been circumspect in recruiting faculty who will be comfortable in an environment not quite like the world at large. On the other hand, a school can capitalize on its possession of or proximity to a rare resource—an observatory, an ecologically unusual location, a superb art collection.

I once interviewed at a school in extreme northern New England, where the head said to me, "You're probably wondering about the cultural life around here. Well, the school *is* the cultural life here." Pondering that information, I did not push my candidacy further; to another interviewee, however, this statement was good news and the position was filled. I was enormously grateful that this head had addressed the area of greatest concern for me as a candidate. This forthrightness saved us both a certain amount of maneuvering. The head might have chosen to gloss over the significant fact of the school's isolation, and I might have found myself a bitter first-year teacher gazing into a bleak New Hampshire winter with little heart or motivation. (On the other hand, I could have been a bit cleverer when applying and saved both of us the trouble of an interview, as the school made little secret of the nature of its location. For someone with a real love of the mountains and the beauty and challenge of a New England winter, this school would have been, and was for many, an ideal situation.)

It is the task of the Hiring Team, then, or some group given the tasks described above, to develop not only the annual "needs assessment" for the recruiting season but also a comprehensive and evolving understanding of the nature of the school itself. Without this specific self-awareness and the ability to articulate it, and to see and take advantage of opportunities as well as to develop compensatory strategies for areas of weakness (like the dating service at the isolated boarding school), the Hiring Team has little hope of connecting the school with the most appropriate and likely candidate pool.

Another task for the Hiring Team in the initial, "pre-season" phase of its work is the development of materials for recruiting candidates. Search committees for heads of school typically spend hours crafting a statement describing the school and its situation, and there is no reason why faculty search documents should not be given the same attention. The image presented in a display ad or an on-line listing is important, whether the school is shopping for a first-grade teacher or a head.

The school's self-description ought to be a model of clarity and integrity, and it should make every effort to include current information of specific interest to teaching candidates. It might be worthwhile for the Hiring Team's to poll recently hired faculty to see what they would want to include in such a document. Information should include location, size, day/boarding, coed/single sex, age or grade levels taught, special religious or philosophical affiliations, and special aspects of the mission. A recounting of a school's history is more important if some aspect of its heritage has been sustained, rather than simply that a future United States president graduated in 1877; this is a place to be informative, not pretentious. Some demographic information about the student body, and even the faculty, is of interest, particularly if that information demonstrates a school's active commitment to racial or socioeconomic diversity or to a population with distinct needs or of a distinct nature. The craft of distilling all this information down to two paragraphs will pay for itself in better candidates.

It must be added here that schools ought to maintain a recruiting and induction budget line item. The Department of Labor and other sources suggest that the cost of replacing an employee can approach or exceed a third of the salary of the departing worker, putting the potential total cost of hiring even an entry-level teacher at something over $10,000; this figure does put placement agency fees in perspective. Clearly, middle management and administrative positions are much more expensive. Note that these estimates include all internal costs associated with turnover, from advertising to interview costs to the multiplicity of benefit-related and other tasks required of business or human resource offices; schools should recognize and account for these items as a significant expense.

As schools cast their nets ever more widely in search of good teaching candidates, many are beginning to prepare specialized materials, including web pages, specifically targeted at telling the school's story to teaching candidates. A small brochure extolling the benefits of teaching at a school can be given out freely at recruiting fairs or sent in acknowledgment of inquiries. A larger document or packet, not unlike (and possibly including) a school's printed viewbook or other student-recruiting admission materials, can be prepared for candidates in whom the school takes a particular interest or to be sent to agencies, college placement offices, or other recruiting portals. The school should not be miserly with such things; good propaganda is good propaganda. (A word of wisdom about format, learned from the listserv of the National Association of College Admission Counselors: promotional materials of non-standard dimensions or unusual form can be annoyances and tend not to be saved or filed, especially if they are too big for a file folder or a standard display rack.)

An increasing number of schools maintain their own job-posting pages ("Careers at," "Employment at") as part of the school website. These pages can be used to promote work at the school and also to provide useful information about the surrounding community or region as well as links to sources on everything from real estate prices to recreational opportunities, local public school systems to restaurants. These links can give prospective candidates a wealth of useful information on which to base decisions about pursuing candidacies that might involve a move. Executive relocation services routinely provide this kind of information as part of business recruitment efforts; schools should be willing to go to the same lengths to attract the best candidates for any and all teaching positions. There is little excuse for recruiting candidates only to lose them to "sticker shock" when they finally get hold of the real estate section of the local newspaper or discover infelicitous details about the public school system to which they would be sending their children. Although the argument can be made that such information is easily found on the Internet and that candidates should be looking after these things on their own, any such service the school can anticipate will pay for itself, as the following story illustrates. An acquaintance in a job search for an administrative position was surprised to find that the school's head had no idea which public school system faculty children attended. Taking this as an indication of the head's interest in the welfare of faculty families, my acquaintance grew increasingly skeptical about the search and eventually withdrew. The school lost a fine candidate because realistic, useful information about the school and the community was not at hand, and my acquaintance took the head's ignorance as emblematic of the school's culture.

A final issue facing the Hiring Team at the outset of its work is simply the identification of openings as they occur. Some school heads are assiduous in anticipating possible departures by early winter, while others seem to let nature take its course. Some schools are casual about the mailing and return of faculty contracts or employment agreements, while others set a firm deadline for their return and devil take the hindmost. In all events, it is imperative that the hiring process begins in as timely a fashion as possible.

Any search should begin with high hopes. In the next chapter we will see how those hopes can be realized.

Best Practices
in Building the Recruiting Case

- Consider hiring the most important part of both program development and institutional advancement.

- Develop a budget line for recruiting and hiring; consider Department of Labor and other estimates of employee replacement cost.

- At the administrative level, identify and reflect on all aspects of school community and culture that relate to faculty work and life: school mission and values; traditions; religious affiliations; politics; workload; faculty demographics with regard to age, gender, ethnicity, sexual orientation, marital/partnership status; geographical considerations; unique assets of the school community.

- Form a Hiring Team to manage the recruitment and hiring process.

- The Hiring Team should consider broad issues relating to school life, including exit interview and teacher departure data; school values and needs; and the characteristics of people who do and do not thrive in the school.

- The Hiring Team should develop an annual "needs assessment" for the school about recruiting and hiring; talking points and common language for recruitment and interviewing; a hiring "master plan" to be updated annually; a strategy for maximizing any advantages the school may have and for addressing disadvantages; and a well-crafted general statement describing the school and its strengths to accompany all position listings and other promotional material used in recruiting.

- Create specific recruiting materials for the school, including a web page, a brochure, and an information packet.

- Provide applicants with detailed information on the nature and assets of school locale: housing; community resources; churches/synagogues/mosques; public schools; cultural resources; natural attractions; and employment opportunities for household members.

Chapter Three
Recruiting

Maxim Three: You can always get what you want.

How often in the spring have you encountered a colleague from another school who is all too ready to tell you that, they are, yup, all hired up for next year—"only had three spots to fill"?

Most of us count these conversations as demoralizing at best. Why did they have only three spots to fill? Where did they get those three great candidates? Anxiety that all the good candidates are gone fills you, and you wonder whether you have overlooked some great résumé that stuck to a piece of junk mail and was tossed out.

I tend to respond to my colleagues' stories with some skepticism. While their schools may have had only three open *teaching* spots, I would be surprised if there were not other holes to fill—coaching, administrative staff, teaching interns. I also have to wonder about the nature of their hires. If I did not see the school represented at diversity recruitment events, for example, I may assume that diversity was not a hiring priority. If I know that the school has some sort of teaching internship program, it crosses my mind that perhaps there were other spots that were filled by interns completing their term of servitude. In all events, if a school makes hiring look too easy, it may not be taking the matter seriously enough.

By now the bias of this book should be clear: that hiring needs to be regarded as a very serious business deserving lavish attention. This is not to say that my colleague's school did not make three hires with extreme efficiency and considerable care—they probably did just that. But the fact is that many schools regard hiring as a checklist item, irksomely consuming hours and attention at a bleak season of the year when there is little enough time to spare from the immediate concerns of the classroom and community morale. It is little wonder that for some schools the best approach to hiring is to get it over with as expeditiously as possible, playing the odds that most of the new people will work out and that there will be a sufficiency of very good ones—real "keepers"—to sustain the quality of the school. Many independent school leaders pride themselves, secretly or not so secretly, on being excellent judges of character (a plausible claim, given that teaching requires us to make judgments of character all the time), and this approach seems, on the whole, to work pretty well.

But I support a more methodical approach to hiring. We have explored the idea that the Hiring Team should be versed not only in the details of the positions that are open but in the nature and needs of the school as an institution that has a mission, a culture, and a set of dreams. We have also considered the simple truth that making a hire can be an act of institutional advancement. Why, then, should the process be seen as only slightly less onerous than filing an income tax return?

As a school and its Hiring Team consider recruiting each new faculty member, they are entitled to hold the highest, most idealistic of aspirations. Why shouldn't the new hiring season be the time to take giant steps toward building a faculty that is diverse in myriad ways, pedagogically creative and expert, and laudable in the individual attainments of its members? Why should not each new teacher offer exactly what is wanted, not a compromise? With intention and effort, a school can indeed have just what it wants, or something very close to it.

The first step in recruiting for a specific position is to develop a concise job description that outlines the basic aspects of the position—teaching tenth-grade American literature, co-teaching in a self-contained third-grade classroom—along with extra duties that might come with the position. These can be stated in general terms, or the description might also note specific requirements—valid state driver's license, hold or be eligible for state certification, knowledge of technology applications in an educational environment, familiar with the common principles of the Coalition of Essential Schools, familiar with the Understanding by Design curriculum model, etc. The listing may include stipulations as to aspects of the position relating to personal characteristics—marital status, physical ability, and, in the case of a religious school, willingness to live and work within a faith-based framework. Preferences or requirements relating to experience may be expressed; a salary range may be specified, or a line such as "salary commensurate with experience" or "competitive salary and benefits" may be included. It is not uncommon to add to position listings a phrase such as "Candidates of color are encouraged to apply."

At some moment, early on, the hiring process shifts from being a matter of planning and strategizing to being a public commitment. The first formal notice of the open position is tacked up on the faculty room bulletin board; the first advertisement is posted on the school's employment website; the first request is passed on to a favorite placement agency or two and to The Green Sheet; the copy for the first display ad is sent to a local or national publication—perhaps Education Week, if the position is significant. The school's "Employment at" brochure is printed or the current information packet is sent to the placement offices of a group of colleges with which the school has had some success, or of which it has some hopes. An individual is designated to post openings on the employment listing pages of a few familiar online sources: the regional independent school association or the NAIS website

By the time this work is done, there should already be a comforting backlog of hopeful, "on spec" résumés and cover letters—some written in very small fonts, indeed—piling up on the desks of department chairs and deans. Most of these, as job seekers who have sent them over the years have learned, will be ignored altogether or at best responded to with a peremptory "will hold" postcard or form letter. While most schools seem to shy away from giving such inquiries much attention, they do at least reassure us that candidates exist, however outré they may be, as evidenced by their eagerness and their apparent failure to register with a placement agency, and that all will be well.

There is something very wrong with the picture that is presented here. Even when the school has the good intentions to send a few people to man a table at an agency job fair in far-off Boston or San Francisco, or even when a few of its administrators will dutifully organize a morning's worth of interviews at the NAIS Annual Conference, and even when the school commits itself to a booth at a couple of diversity recruiting events, there is a kind of passivity, an attitude of "wait and see what drops into our laps" or of going once again to the same old well.

There are schools that hire only through agencies, preferring to let the agency staff do the initial vetting and interviewing of candidates and working from the agencies' paragraph summaries much as they would shop from an L. L. Bean catalogue: known quality, excellent customer service. This is certainly a great convenience, even at the relatively high premium charged by the agency as its fee. Many schools work with several agencies, having found a comfort zone that works for them.

There are schools that really do dismiss unsolicited inquiries out of hand, preferring to work only through agencies and through networks of friends and acquaintances; my own informal survey suggests that well over half of beginning teachers in New England come to their positions via one of these two routes. I have encountered independent school people who say that they would never hire a former public school teacher, or that they would be extremely uncomfortable hiring a middle-aged career-changer.

Each school will have to come to terms on its own with how to treat "non-traditional" applicants, but it is important that the Hiring Team understand the nature of any traditional "prejudices" the school may have. If career-changing applicants in their middle years are unappealing simply because of their unfamiliarity with the culture and demands of independent schools, then there needs to be a discussion of how that unfamiliarity could be overcome; many truly great teachers have found their second wind and true calling after spending years toiling in other vineyards. Some schools love having the cachet and expertise of PhDs on the faculty, but others worry that the work ethic of long-term graduate students may not be up to the demands of pre-collegiate teaching. The school must openly consider the extent to which such preconceptions limit its own possibilities.

A number of independent schools have established some form of referral incentive program in which a teacher who directs a candidate to the school who is ultimately hired receives some form of bonus, running as high as a thousand dollars for a full-time position. The advantage of such a program is that faculty know the school's work environment, and they can also give acquaintances the "inside scoop."

This helps ensure that candidates referred by faculty are at least plausible as employees, but it is important, once the referral has been made, that there is no special favor given to the candidate beyond that which they earn through qualifications and character. It should go without saying that an individual making a referral who is part of the hiring process should not be eligible for any sort of reward or bonus. Schools might even consider weighing fully the risks of establishing a culture of favoritism or cronyism. Referral programs can work well as a midpoint between an old boys' and girls' network and a more open process, but there is always the risk that a faculty member whose friend is not hired will in the end feel antipathy toward the school.

Another situation fraught with the potential for hurt feelings and much worse involves the promotion or reassignment of internal candidates. "Open" searches that turn out to have had predetermined outcomes or searches that no one even knew about until the announcement is made that a position has been filled can create real animosity. A faculty should not be given reason to feel unsure about how hiring decisions, and in particular promotions, are made. This should not prevent a school from acting to meet its needs, but the process of internal promotion and reassignment should be made as transparent as possible.

The point is, schools have their ways, and these ways can sometimes constrict the flow of teaching candidates to the inner sanctum where job offers occur, or can create unforeseen difficulties in the community. By acting expediently rather than strategically, many schools do get what they want in a practical sense, but do not necessarily achieve their highest hopes.

A more promising approach to hiring involves both a more broad-based campaign to promulgate news of the school's openings and a more tightly focused program to seek out and win over precisely the applicants the school wants to attract.

Even a tight recruiting budget will have room for a modest expansion of print advertising. Look locally through newspapers—you may attract a candidate who is already established in the area. If you are actively interested in hiring for racial or cultural diversity, make a point of finding out which regional publications and websites serve particular populations, and advertise there. Along with the possibility of finding a great teacher, you will also be making a public statement to that community of your school's interest in serving it, a statement that may pay dividends in other ways. Post an advertisement in local or regional GLBTQ publications. If you are interested in hiring experienced teachers, be so bold as to take out an ad in the newsletter of your local or state public school teachers union. In each case, the community outreach is in itself a worthy effort. But do not, of course, squander the capital you acquire by then neglecting to respond to each applicant who contacts the school from these sources.

Similarly, subject-matter or age-level specialists can be found through various professional organizations, online and in print. Most of the national associations of subject matter teachers (the National Council of Teachers of English, the American Council on the Teaching of Foreign Language, the National Council for the Social Studies, the National Council of Teachers of Mathematics, for example) or age-level educators (the National Middle School Association, the National Association for the Education of Young Children) maintain job posting pages on their websites; some, however, require payment of a listing fee. The H-NET listserv maintains a pay-for-listing job site. Other listservs, too, permit listing of positions: the Independent School Educators list ("ISED-L"); the list the National Association for College Admission Counseling, LM_NET (for library/media specialists);; and the NAIS Connect on-line communities. Most of these electronic sites require no more than "sweat equity," a relatively small price to pay for the exposure gained. Education Week maintains a for-pay site, as well. Additional resources can be found through a quick Internet search.

Another resource, little known to independent school educators but potentially useful, is Troops to Teachers, a U.S. Department of Defense program aimed at placing in teaching positions individuals who are leaving the military. Registration and listings are free and easy to manage—another sweat equity resource. It also is possible to connect with Teach for America. While TFA is not wild about attrition, the reality is that some participants in the program do opt out after their first year of the two-year commitment, but many wish to stay in teaching. TFA veterans have had training as well as experience in a variety of settings, some of them quite challenging.

Some independent schools offer teaching apprenticeship or internship programs that provide serious training. Most such programs do not subsequently hire all, or even any, of their own trainees, and so graduates of programs such as those at the Progressive Education Lab and Shady Hill School are available—trained and experienced. Even more schools offer internship programs that are more like entry level, part-time beginning teaching jobs; often these programs have exposed participants to a variety of situations. Although the intent of such programs may not be to offer intensive teacher training, participants who elect to remain in the field may bring solid experience. The best way to find schools with internship programs is to post a query on an appropriate listserv or to inquire of a regional independent school association.

Other excellent resources, although expensive, are job fairs and employment fairs. Regional associations sponsor some of these, but there are other kinds of fairs as well. College placement offices sometimes sponsor such events, as do local or statewide chambers of commerce. Career fairs are a part of the fabric of life in the technology industry; a table at one of these might drum up a candidate in science or mathematics as well as a technology specialist. Schools can make the most of job fairs by good preparation: promotional materials; careful perusal of any preliminary candidate information supplied by sponsors; and most importantly some previously scripted talking points and questions for candidates (see Chapter Four).

It is worth remembering that there are good, experienced people out there who are not satisfied in their careers but who may not understand or know very much about independent schools. For individuals for whom the career "itch" is about wanting a working environment in which personal connections are paramount, the news about independent school teaching could be life changing.

Placing classroom teachers in jobs one-by-one might not be worth the time of executive-placement services that work for a percentage of salary, but a group of schools or a regional independent schools association might sponsor an event for career-counseling specialists. Using the NAIS materials and first-person stories, as well as some factual materials from the schools themselves, the event could focus on explaining what independent school teaching is all about and how their clients might explore the field.

The independent school community has to deal with a still-pervasive sense that "marketing," whether advertising the school for enrollment management purposes or for recruiting faculty, is somehow tasteless and even a little bit crass. It is difficult to imagine how posting job listings in any likely venue exposes a school to charges of shameless self-promotion; perhaps there are schools who are hesitant to admit their need to hire teachers from time to time. In the face of the ongoing need for new blood in the independent school teaching profession, this reluctance seems wrongheaded and more than a little bit elitist and prissy—smacking of, "If you have to be told of our existence, you can't really belong to the club." In the meantime, schools that are not afraid to work a little harder to connect their needs with potential candidates will be hiring some great teachers.

In some regions a few independent schools have elected to be acknowledged on-air as supporters of local public radio stations, a strategy that seems quite cleverly aimed at alerting just the right demographic to the existence of the school and its programs. It would be interesting to learn whether adding to the name of the school the tag line something like "offering exciting and rewarding careers to experienced and beginning teachers" might also attract a teaching candidate or two—people who would bring an awareness of the world that would be an addition to any faculty.

Because most independent schools have the luxury of not requiring certification or licensure for their teachers, the reality is that teachers can come from almost any background. Schools should recognize the magnitude of the opportunity this presents. Individuals with good-quality undergraduate or graduate degrees in academic subjects, some work experience, and either a passionate desire or a growing hankering to work with young people are not as rare as they might seem. But they do not all know about the big teacher placement service agencies or the old boys' and girls' networks or even NAIS. There is no shortage of places in which an advertisement or some other notice of a job opening might reach someone who has never quite considered independent school teaching or whose knowledge of "the system" is unsophisticated. In some cases, these are just the candidates that are both wanted and needed to build stronger, better schools and more effective learning environments for students.

COROLLARY A: There is no excuse for failing at diversity.

Virtually all independent schools voice a commitment to diversity. But in relatively few independent schools does this commitment manifest itself in the people on its faculty. Only a handful of schools, even those in which student racial and cultural diversity is broad and deep, have been able to match that diversity in the matter of hiring faculty.

If your school has been working on this issue, you may read this as an accusation, or at least with a certain frustrated guilt. Many, many schools have been making a good faith effort to increase faculty diversity for some time, and all of those schools would agree that recruiting a diverse faculty is a serious and difficult challenge. They are correct. The schools that have found real success have had to make some real changes in their overall approach to faculty recruitment.

The degree to which hiring for diversity is a school priority must be clear at the outset of the hiring process, and the school's recruiting efforts should be focused to a high degree on attracting a pool of candidates representing the kinds of diversity being sought. This is a matter for serious consideration and careful institutional design. One way in which a school can proactively represent a commitment to diversity is to develop a hiring policy or set of policies and procedures that contain specific goals. For example, many schools maintain a policy that an offer for any position will not be tendered until there has been at least one finalist candidate of color seen and given a full hearing as part of the hiring process.

The objections to maintaining such a policy—especially when a search is undertaken late in the year—are that it may "slow things down," or that "there just aren't that many candidates out there." Both of these may seem valid to a degree, but the school's response must be to expand the breadth of recruitment efforts, even into non-traditional areas, in order to identify more applicants. A school that holds itself to a high standard about such a policy makes clear to candidates and to its community the seriousness of its intent to build a particular kind of institution. Moreover, it can be argued that a longer but more deliberate search will improve the quality of the candidate pool as a whole—even, it may be said, into July.

Some might claim that a hiring policy focused on diversity is a kind of racially preferential "affirmative action" as the notion is understood in the conservative media. It absolutely is not. This process is not about taking a position or an opportunity away from anyone. It can be argued that independent schools have an opportunity and even an obligation to sustain the possibilities of creating a diverse society. An irony in the history of American independent education is that, even with its early heritage as elitist, today independent schools represent a kind of utopianism—an effort to create intentional communities based on chosen, specific, and articulated values and goals. The effort to build diverse communities that value a multicultural outlook is another step in the evolution of this aspiration. The moral imperatives of our time include expanding the equity of access and opportunity in all spheres of experience. Schools should be inspired to act. This is not about conforming to a politically correct agenda or about window dressing. Schools, even those whose student body and community are primarily white, must embrace this imperative and reject out of hand any tendency to excuse themselves from carrying it out.

The greatest challenges, of course, face those schools that truly cut off geographically from the real racial and cultural diversity that now defines urban/suburban North America and most of the rural/exurban South, West Coast, and Southwest. The programmatic problem for such schools is to create what may be called a kind of virtual diversity—the representation of multicultural viewpoints through curricular content and initiatives, through assiduous training of faculty, and, where possible, by bringing these viewpoints into the community in the person of presenters, teachers, administrators, and trustees. Virtual diversity depends on the proactive good will of the school's leaders and families, on the open acknowledgment of white privilege and its manifestations, and on understanding the need to teach students to look at the world from a multiplicity of viewpoints.

If a school's reasonable geographical pool of applicant students does not include significant diversity, it has all the more reason to make extraordinary efforts to develop a diverse faculty. It is clear enough that an added challenge here is to entice a person to join a community in which their racial or cultural "difference" will be significantly more apparent simply as a matter of contrast. This does not mean that the school can give up; it may even mean that the school should actively engage in the recruitment of a number of faculty from underrepresented groups, thus perhaps developing a community that could be the beginning of a broader base of diversity in a hitherto monocultural area.

The matter of recruiting a diverse faculty is critical on a number of levels. How to do it is, once again, a matter of some added effort and a modest expenditure. I have already mentioned the value of minority publications and websites for posting teaching openings, and earlier in this chapter referred to job fairs and their utility. Some regional independent school associations regularly sponsor job fairs focused on minority hiring, as do such organizations as the National Employment Minority Network, better known as NEMNET. Independent schools should seek any opportunity to connect with the placement offices of historically black colleges and universities to post listings or to participate in job fairs. Once again, such connections not only serve to help schools meet their own needs but also to make a statement of their aspirations and values. (It is a truism that many minority students who hope to enter teaching point themselves toward public school systems as a way of "giving back." A sometimes compelling answer to this is that independent schools are attracting increasing numbers of minority students who need role models and that relatively privileged white students need to experience authoritative adults who represent cultures and races other than their own.)

NAIS can also be a valuable resource for schools seeking to recruit faculty. The association's website has a page devoted to placement services, and minority recruitment in particular. NAIS can advise schools on the development of programs and policies related to all aspects of diversity, equity, and multiculturalism and will support the ongoing development of a community in which students and faculty of color alike are active, engaged, and valued members. Because "diversity," of course, is only a first step. The faces in the school picture represent the human and cultural foundation on which the community is built. Multiculturalism, the enactment of values based on the recognition, exchange, and celebration of cultural difference, is the goal, and faculty recruitment is an extremely important aspect of that enactment.

COROLLARY B: There is no excuse for intentionally hiring cannon fodder.

Schools need to hire educators. Too often, it is a convenience for schools to hire recent college graduates who are little more than live bodies with credible résumés whose task is do a bit of teaching—often introductory or low-level courses—as they bring their youthful energy and other useful skills to the school. These may include coaching, based perhaps on some experience as a college or even high school athlete, and dormitory supervision, based on little more than a willingness to exchange the stresses of apartment hunting for room, board, and the rigors of supervising a wing full of 15-year-olds.

Many of these young people bring a bright, positive demeanor to their work, perhaps stemming from happy summers spent as camp counselors or their own inspiring experiences as boarding school students. But these fine young people—and they are fine young people for the most part—are in fact the cannon fodder of independent school teaching. Those who hire them have few illusions that they will stay for long, and, other than that most of them have done well at selective colleges, they bring little special interest in education as an activity, a field of study, or as a profession. For many of them, teaching at an independent school is intended to be a challenging but ulti- mately enjoyable interlude while they ponder more permanent career choices; some may even have sufficient independent means not to be overly concerned with matters of salary and benefits.

Each year's new crop of "triple threat" youngsters—eager, talented, and for the most part not representing a great deal of diversity—includes a few who will turn out to be spectacularly talented classroom teachers. Many will be excellent coaches or assistant coaches, and most will survive life in the dormitory with only a few bumps and bruises. Almost all will be inspiring and even memorable mentors to at least a couple of students. A small number will prove unsuitable or will be unable to restrain their own lifestyles. They will disappear quietly or not so quietly as the year goes by. Many will spend their late nights boning up on GRE, LSAT, GMAT, or MCAT questions. They will do their jobs to the best of their ability.

Some schools make a real investment in their young Jacks and Jills of all trades. They enroll them in regional associations' pre-service programs that take place early in the school year. They establish their own induction and mentoring programs that have real substance and that devote real time—and some resources—in making effective teachers out of their rookies. Schools that have done these things, and that have seen the need to develop all members of their faculties as professional educators, are to be commended. But unless these schools see themselves as training educators, as opposed to making the most out of a transient and interchangeable population, they contribute at least a little to the "cannon fodder" mentality that has for too long viewed these freshly scrubbed young faces with prestigious degrees as a fungible, cheap commodity on the teacher market.

No school should ever set out to look for teachers who are only intended to fill spots. Of course schools will need to recruit triple threats until the end of time, but this recruiting should be done with an attitude toward, if you will, improving the breed. The aim of all independent schools should be to develop as many young people as possible into real educators, professionals who can take pride in their skills, in their efficacy as role models and mentors to all their charges, and in the respect they are given as professionals by peers, by students and their families, by the institutions in which they work, and by the world at large.

The Hiring Team, then, must embody, along with the hopes and needs of the school, a higher set of dreams. The teachers recruited into any given school are representatives not only of the highest ideals of independent schools as conscious instruments of social progress and a higher morality but also of the professionalism and professional standing of all teachers. The obligation on the Hiring Team and on the school as a whole is not to lose sight of these great goals even as they struggle with the minutiae of the hiring process.

Best Practices
in Recruiting

- Have high expectations for each position to be filled, and expend the resources and time to meet those expectations.

- Develop concise, clear job descriptions for each open position, and include important stipulations—experience, training, physical or marital preferences—in each listing.

- Cast the widest net possible: print and community media; placement agencies; college placement offices; specialized publications or other media (subject-area listservs or websites, publications for individuals with particular ethnicities, racial backgrounds, or sexual orientations); online listing sites; and likely sources of experienced or trained teachers (Troops-to-Teachers, Teach for America). Consider using non-traditional approaches (support of public radio, employee referral programs).

- Be alert to the need for transparency in the treatment of internal candidates or decisions to create and fill new positions from within without posting them.

- Attend job fairs and take them seriously as opportunities to present the school;

have excellent materials and a focused interview strategy.

- Design a tracking log to keep tabs on all applicants.
- Consider developing a hiring policy relating to diversity, and hold tightly to that policy, even if it takes time.
- Target diversity hiring efforts specifically—NEMNET, HBCUs; use NAIS resources.
- Check the One Schoolhouse Independent Curriculum webinar archive for webinars related to teacher recruiting, hiring, and retention.
- Approach each hire as a lifetime appointment; don't settle for less than what the school needs most, even if it takes time; remember the high real cost of employee replacement.
- Be prepared to offer pre-service training as a way of bringing new hires with great potential but skill gaps up to speed.

Chapter Four
Hiring

Maxim Four: It takes a
school to hire a teacher.

It is hard to say precisely what chemistry leads to the offer of a teaching position and then to its acceptance. Some combination of working conditions, school culture, salary and benefits, and personal connections brings each search to a happy conclusion. What is clear, however, is that the most satisfying and long-lasting relationships between teachers and schools commence during the hiring process. To lay the groundwork for these relationships, a school should put its best foot forward and learn what there is to learn about each candidate.

The keys to making this part of the process work well are organization, frankness, and above all, clear lines of communication from school to candidate. While one person may provide the spark that seals the deal, the entire school must ensure that the deal is ready for signature in the first place.

This may seem like the kind of administrivia that can drape a wet blanket over even the best laid plans, but as soon as a school begins to receive letters about teaching positions, some person or some office needs to be designated as the central repository for inquiries. This designated spot—"hiring central"—may also be the single contact name, specified in all advertisements and postings, to whom inquiries are to be directed. The establishment of hiring central is essential, because the potential for chaos and the alienation or outright loss of good candidates is otherwise unacceptably high. Initial inquiries and unsolicited résumés will arrive addressed to any number of offices and individuals—some of them long departed. Unless the materials are consolidated at one destination, the chance of their being read and given the appropriate attention diminishes. A name or coded office title and a designated e-mail address ("employment@yourschool.org") will direct reasonably well-researched or specific inquiries to the right place.

If a school is large enough to have its own human resources office or function, then hiring central already exists. Typically, inquiries might otherwise be directed to a dean of faculty or a specific administrative staff office; large schools or schools with separate campuses might choose to do this by division. A school in which hiring occurs autonomously by department ought still to process inquiries in a centralized, school-wide manner to make sure that certain courtesies are observed and that candidates with multiple talents are seen by all who need to.

For each hiring season the school should establish a tracking log listing each applicant's name, the date of receipt of materials, and the applicant's particular areas of interest (a simple code will suffice). Although this may involve hundreds of letters at some schools, the reason is not only to keep track of potentially strong candidates but also to make sure that all applicants will be treated with civility—*any* inquiry the school receives from a job seeker merits the courtesy of an acknowledgment. The simplest response is a postcard thanking the applicant for their interest and stating that materials will be held on file while the school's needs are being assessed and that the school may contact them at a later date, etc. These postcards can be printed up well in advance and addressed and dated as needed. A boilerplate e-mail conveying the same message could also be held for origination from the "employment" e-mail account. The card or e-mail should be sent as soon as possible in response to any inquiry. (It might be gilding the lily to do so, but a school could also respond to unsolicited or unspecified inquiries by sending not only the postcard but also a form letter along with any basic information related to employment—a brochure or simply a fact sheet.)

Why, in this age of instant communication when a poorly researched inquiry is almost embarrassing to the recipient, should a school go to the trouble and expense of acknowledging every single résumé that comes through the door? Because it is the right thing, the polite thing, to do. Failure to do so reflects poorly upon the school. I could still tell you the names of the two schools that did not acknowledge my first job-search letter over forty years ago. I have long since forgiven, but I have not forgotten. Does it matter in the great scale of things? No. But it matters considerably in the small scale.

The tracking log ought also to specify, again by code, how the applicant came by the knowledge of the opening. Are college placement listings, or print or on-line advertisements paying off? Unless there is an attempt to track this, the information will be lost.

The Hiring Team should spell out the protocol by which inquiries will be processed. This should include two special categories of applicant: those met at job fairs and those whose papers have been forwarded by a third party, such as a placement agency or college placement office. School representatives at job fairs should keep track of all candidates with whom they had more than cursory conversations; this should of course include candidates with whom the school actively solicited conversations. Papers forwarded directly from a placement agency do not require response. However, if the candidate submits a specific letter of interest on their own, acknowledge it.

The protocol stipulating the flow of papers through hiring central should be clear to everyone. If the first vetting is to be done by an administrator (a dean, a division director, or even a head of school) rather than by the direct supervisor of the position (a department head or division director), everyone should understand this and know the approximate timetable for completing the review. If the supervisor is the first reader, with promising papers then being upstreamed to an administrative office, make that clear. The hiring log should show the order in which papers will be reviewed, and most importantly it should allow each step to be checked off as it is completed, as well noting the disposition—no further action (file), hold through a specific date for future need, contact for interview—or whatever steps and categories are appropriate for the school and its needs. Most importantly, put papers that warrant further action into a file folder—color-coded, perhaps, to indicate that the file is active—and give them to the person responsible for the next step.

What that step is depends on a number of factors, including the school's budget, the whereabouts of the candidate, the school's urgency about filling the position, or the attractiveness of the candidate. In all events, it involves some form of direct contact with the candidate. This may involve a designated representative of hiring central inviting the candidate to the school for an interview via a telephone call or even e-mail. Ideally, there should be a "live" conversation, even if e-mail is used to schedule a good time to call; the personal touch begins here.

A very serious caveat: At the point of the first live contact between the school and a candidate, the school becomes subject to the laws related to equal employment opportunity. There are questions and approaches that must not be asked or taken, and only some thoughtful training for EVERYONE who will have contact with candidates can assure that the hiring process will proceed within the letter and the spirit of the law. Your school's attorney, a regional association attorney, or (easiest and probably least expensive) a four-hour On Demand course, "Interviewing and Hiring," offered by the National Business Officers Association through One Schoolhouse) can help keep your school in full compliance.

At one point early in my career I was asked to visit a school that had no specific openings in my area and where none were anticipated. The very experienced head simply made a practice of doing a few interviews "on spec" every now and then. The February interview was no more than a get-acquainted session; I was both flattered to learn that my short résumé had been interesting enough to attract attention and dismayed that not much was likely to come of it. Nonetheless, I enjoyed my visit. When the school called me in midsummer to tell me that a position had suddenly opened up I was delighted to return as a real candidate; I spent three very happy years at the school. Perhaps I'm biased, but I see great value to a school in developing a small reserve of interesting potential candidates even when no specific need exists.

Some schools prefer to preface an actual school visit with a brief telephone conversation that may or may not be an interview. This might simply be a way of gauging whether a faraway candidate should be brought to the school for a formal interview or it might be considered a formal part of the process, given the weight of an initial conversation at a job fair.

School representatives at job fairs as well as first-round interviewers in telephone or face-to-face contexts will find it useful to have a script, carefully vetted to ensure compliance with employment law, both of talking points about the school and of a few specific questions that are asked of all candidates. At the early stage of the process the need is to develop data about prospective teachers that can be used in a way that allows the comparison of apples to apples—how Candidates A and B respond to the same question. These questions could be developed by the Hiring Team or by the department or division to which the candidate is applying. Consistency is the key.

The structured interview format can save time and help interviewers keep conversations focused on aspects of the candidate's interest, background, and personal qualities that relate specifically to the job. At the point of first contact with a candidate, the benefits of the practice seem clear.

At some point the preliminary work is done and it is time to invite a few candidates to the school. Here again, clarity about the overall process and the visit structure is crucial, both to the candidate and to all those involved in the hire. If the on-campus interview is intended to be a one-and-only event, a finale, it should be as broad-based and inclusive as possible. If two or even three visits are anticipated before a decision is made, the staging of each should be set forth before the first is made.

If there is a Law of Hiring, it is that a candidate can never be given too much information or given that information too soon. The legitimate anxiety of the candidate to know where they stand at each point in the process can never be completely alleviated, but to leave a candidate hanging at any stage of the process is a small act of cruelty. If there is a delay in the process, tell the candidate. A detailed explanation is not required, but the candidate should know what to expect next and approximately when. It should be someone's specific task to maintain contact with the candidate; that person should consider the candidate's point of view in the effort to keep them both informed and feeling positive about the school and its process.

A sometimes-sticky issue can arise relating to candidate travel expenses. The candidate should be told the school's policy at the beginning: Will the school cover all travel or a portion? What is the reimbursement process, and the timetable for it? Some schools will not pay for travel except for a candidate who is a finalist; others reimburse at a set rate (the lowest published carrier fare, for example, or the Federal government employee rate). Schools in metropolitan areas may be able to share the travel costs of a candidate who is interviewing at several schools. In all events, clarity and communication are essential.

If more than a single on-campus interview is planned, the candidate's first visit may include only a limited number of office interviews, and no special arrangements need be made for these. At least a short tour should occur on a first visit, a chance for the candidate to see some of the campus and acquire a feel for the school—how it looks, how it acts, what the energy level is like.

If the school visit is to be a full-dress affair, it should be carefully orchestrated. Some schools will ask a candidate to prepare a sample lesson to be taught in the actual classroom in which the teacher would be working if hired; obviously, sufficient notice is needed for this. As much as possible, the school should work to make the "major" visit schedule as uniform as possible for all candidates, once again to ensure that when decision time arrives the comparisons are of apples to apples.

What writing exists on the subject of teacher interviews suggests strongly that the days of the visit to the department chair and then the head should be over. While some schools persist in the notion that the only judgment that matters is that of the school, as embodied in a couple of leaders, these days the marketplace is such that the school needs to sell itself. The candidate has to like the prospects before them.

Because teachers are expected to take on many roles—classroom teacher, advisor, activity leader, possibly residential supervisor—the candidate ought to meet with a few, if not all, of those in charge of these areas. Because in the end most of a teacher's time will be spent with students, there ought to be some opportunity for the candidate to meet with at least a few of them—as tour guides, over lunch, or perhaps even in a more formal setting. (Students who meet with candidates need to understand their role: to be themselves and to give the candidate an idea of life at the school from the student point of view. Whatever role their reaction to the candidate will have in the decision-making process should be made clear to them at the outset.) Because understanding and valuing the principles of multiculturalism is a critical skill in independent education, the diversity office should be included in the interview process. It is wise to allow time for a candidate of color or an openly LGBTQ candidate an opportunity to meet with someone who can candidly represent what life at the school is like for faculty of color or gay or lesbian teachers.

Whoever is on the "interview circuit"—probably members of the Hiring Team, the division or department head, and perhaps another one or two—should at some point get together to discuss at least in general terms the kinds of questions they are likely to ask candidates and the qualities they are looking for. Although the full-scale interview should be scheduled but not scripted, it is useful for everyone to be aware of the interests and propensities of their fellow interviewers.

When the meetings are concluded, all interviewers should have a common response form to be returned to hiring central as soon as possible. This could be as simple as an assessment of strengths and weaknesses and further thoughts, or it could be a scoring rubric. Simple is better, as brevity increases the chances of the response form actually being returned. Some schools may wish to end the form with a category recommending action—hire, wait, do not hire—but it may facilitate better discussions later if such recommendations are not made, at least formally, at this time.

The matter of the sample class—a more common phenomenon at the elementary and middle levels than in high schools—is more complicated. There are several drawbacks to this process, not the least of which is that a fumblingly nervous applicant may in fact be a fine teacher—but you will never know that. An applicant looking for their first job will not necessarily have a repertoire of ideas or even much more than an intuitive idea of lesson planning. Strong objections could also be raised to making students the guinea pigs for lessons of unpredictable quality. On the other hand, the school will see the candidate doing what teachers do and learn at least something about their manner with students and ability to think on their feet. In addition, some jittery candidates are calmed by immersion in their own element. How a sample lesson is to be evaluated, and by whom, is a question that the school must answer before setting it up. A very simple rubric based on the school's values or articulated standards of effective teaching might be in order.

The visit should also include interludes of down time for the candidate—to eat, to sip a cup of coffee, to visit the rest room, or even just to reflect or jot down questions. Although it is not inhumane to schedule a very busy day for the candidate, the day should not be an endurance test. How the school chooses to make candidates feel welcome and comfortable will depend on a number of local and human factors, but the point is that candidates *should* feel welcome and comfortable—not as if they are either on trial or should be considering themselves as humble supplicants before the awesome majesty of the school. A school that is too magisterial, sending the message that "It is the highest of all privileges to work here, and you probably are not worthy" will lose good candidates, no matter how august and prestigious it may be.

For the actual question-and-answer part of the interview, the interviewers should make sure that all the appropriate ground is covered: details about relevant experience; reasons for wanting to teach and in particular in this school; incidents in life that developed motivation or interest; outside interests; questions about subject matter knowledge or pedagogical expertise. Some interviewers like to set forth scenarios or to inquire about best or hardest professional moments; others like to learn as much as possible about the personal preferences and character of the candidate.

As referenced above in our exhortation to have all interviewers (down to tour guides, if necessary) trained in the legal aspects of "interviewing," there are a number of categories of proscribed questions and topics that can expose an unwary or insensitive interviewer to problems both ethical and legal. A candidate can be under no compulsion whatsoever to identify or discuss their race, religion, ethnicity, sexual orientation, age, use of prescription or illegal drugs, marital or partnership status, health issues, or disability, although stipulations about the latter three—and the use of illegal substances—may be laid out in the job description as conditions of employment. A school can ask for pre-employment drug testing or physical examinations, but such requests should probably be made as a blanket policy rather than on a case-by-case basis. As case law in these areas is complex, schools puzzling over specific issues should consult their own counsel as well as the many resources on employment law available through NAIS. The safest course is to go only by what is either stated by a candidate or is specified in the résumé. A candidate who appears to be of color may not so self identify (and vice versa). To make assumptions about other aspects of a person's background or the "categories" into which they fall is to swim in legally and morally dangerous waters.

Related to the proscriptions around interview questions is the matter of reference and criminal background checks. That any school would make an offer to a candidate without having checked references or that any offer would not be conditional upon the results of a criminal background investigation is inconceivable—and yet it happens. While many candidates supply written references—standard procedure in placement agency packets—others will supply only a list of references and contact information. Some candidates may have to be reminded to provide this information. In all events, it must be the responsibility of someone at the school to perform a check that represents "due diligence" insofar as it protects the school, and above all, its students.

Reference checks should be made *viva voce*, most often by telephone. As in the case of candidate interviews, there are topics that may not be broached by the questioner—age, race, religion, sexual orientation—but questions specifically related to job performance are fine. These might include punctuality, length of employment, reliability, observed effectiveness, and reasons for departure. Fishing for negatives is acceptable but may not bear fruit—or it may make the reference ill at ease and thus close off useful lines of inquiry. Questions asked and statements made in a reference conversation ought to be regarded as confidential; this may be so stated by the questioner at the beginning of the conversation. Unfortunately, there can be no guarantee in this area.

A reference who is exceedingly cautious, legalistically precise, or extremely circumspect in responding to questions may simply be being judicious out of a general sense of legal vulnerability. But there may be more serious issues behind the reticence. It is up to the parties in the conversation to work out how much information will be conveyed. A reference who is reluctant to share specific negative information may be able to respond discreetly to carefully crafted yes-or-no questions, but sometimes the questioner is left with more questions than information. Employers are becoming very lawsuit-minded in their handling of reference calls, and a number may be willing only to confirm dates of employment. Such employers may be willing to supply information of attendance, punctuality, or reliability, but only in response to specific questions as to the candidate's record in those areas.

Obviously, references from friends and relatives of the candidate need to be taken as what they are, and in many cases references from college or graduate school professors do not provide much information of great relevance to teaching. References from high school teachers can be useful if the candidate has stayed in touch and if the referrer knows about the candidate's interest in and suitability for teaching. A college coach or activity supervisor with whom the candidate has worked closely may be very aware of character and work ethic. What you can hope to learn from any reference call is that the candidate is reliable, honest, knowledgeable, and personally up to the challenges of teaching and other duties in a school. References that cannot address these areas are not of much use, and references that will not address these areas are probably raising red flags. It is important to understand that the circumstances of your school are in some ways unique, and those who have to make the hiring decision must ultimately determine how much weight to give to problematic areas that surface in the reference process.

Criminal background investigations are required for all teachers in some states, and ***due diligence demands that some form*** *of check be done whether or not it is mandated*. Some states have a simple procedure for requesting records, and there are also third-party entities that will undertake more exhaustive investigations for a fee. A school that at the very least fails to check the driving record of anyone who will be driving students, either in school vehicles or their own cars, is exposing itself to legal difficulties. Here again, the complexities of case law and variations in jurisdictional requirements suggest that school counsel be consulted on specific issues. Then, too, school personnel will have to determine how to interpret the inevitable surprises that show up when such checks are done: Is a fine for disorderly conduct at a college hockey game a deal-breaker, or excusable high spirits? Does a drug possession charge that was dismissed in 1993 indicate moral turpitude?

Reference checks may be initiated as soon as it is clear that a candidate is a finalist, even before a last interview. This will make it possible for an offer to be made without delay—even as the culmination of a final interview, if an agreement can be reached quickly among those deciding on the hire. The background investigation can wait, but the offer of employment should be clearly provisional until the results are in. A school may wish to do further research, as well, checking academic credentials or military service records. The expense may well be worth saving the school some later embarrassment. A school that has once been burned in this area will thereafter perform credential checks as a matter of course.

How the decision is reached on making an offer will vary by school and sometimes by situation. In an ideal world all those who have interviewed all candidates meet to discuss the virtues of each, interview response forms are reviewed and reference conversations are recounted, a consensus is reached, and whoever is empowered to make the offer does so. Often, however, the enthusiasm of the moment seizes the group in response to a spectacularly strong interview, hurried consultations are made, and the die is cast. As long as there is clarity and all parties have been communicated with—and references checked!—this process is likely to work well. In the opposite case, when interview after interview seems to yield no candidate about whom there is a generally positive feeling, there may come a point when some serious discussions of criteria and judgments must take place and a decision whether to extend the search must be made.

If the Hiring Team has a mandate regarding specific criteria—the requirement that there be a finalist of color before an offer can be made, for example—then patience becomes a virtue and efforts to achieve the goal must be redoubled. That is all there is to it; there can be no letting the school off the hook. If you need to go back to the recruiting effort, so be it.

Making an offer can be a single-stage or two-stage process, depending on whether the initial conversation includes the discussion of salary and benefits. If the issue has been raised during the interviews, the candidate should have a good idea what the range is likely to be, but it may be that the conversation begins cold. To what degree negotiation is possible will vary from school to school, as will the amount of time the candidate is given to reply. Each year many schools lose good candidates because of the deadline for responding to another offer; in the end these things probably even out. But they are worth tracking. If the Hiring Team finds that the school is consistently losing candidates in this way, action needs to taken to streamline the process of making offers.

Finalists who are ultimately not offered jobs should be treated to a personalized communication, preferably by telephone; make a serious attempt not to leave a voicemail message, especially (absolutely, really) if you know that the candidate shares a telephone line with a housemate or partner. A personal letter is the next best thing; e-mail, like voice-mail, is a coward's way out and should not be used. If there is some personal relationship, new or old, between the administrator responsible for delivering bad news and a disappointed candidate, it might be all right to invite further contact to discuss the decision. Otherwise it is best to thank the candidate, explain that the decision has been made to take the search in a different direction, comment positively on some aspect of the candidacy, wish the candidate good luck, and cut the cord cleanly—personal, direct, humane, and done with integrity, moral courage, and class.

Once the last offer has been made and accepted, it would be worthwhile for the Hiring Team to get together to review the year's operations. If there is a general sense of frustration, there is work to be done; in severe situations it might even be worth polling lost or withdrawn candidates to learn how the process might be improved or what factors ultimately discouraged the candidate from pursuing the job. If the process went particularly well, the new hires should also be asked for some feedback as to positive areas that could be further enhanced in the future.

The Hiring Team may then congratulate itself on a job well done. More importantly, every member of the school community with whom any candidate had even the slightest contact—a nod, a smile, or a half-hour conversation—played a significant role in making that hire happen. It was not just the department head or the head of school; it was the faculty, the students, and the staff. There should be genuine excitement throughout the school about the new teachers, an excitement that has been well earned. Now the school's marketing and communication machinery should be gearing up to communicate this excitement to the rest of the school family, and, as soon as possible, the new hires should be brought into that family in a positive and supportive way

Best Practices in Hiring

- Establish "hiring central": a person or office to manage the hiring process and through whom or which all paperwork will flow.

- Use the tracking log to manage inquiries and responses; be sure to track the sources of applicants' interest in the school.

- Respond to every inquiry, even the most unlikely; include job fair interviewees in this; a simple "thank you" will suffice.

- Develop a protocol for the flow of candidate papers; make sure everyone understands the process.

- Consider interviewing interesting candidates "on spec," even if no position is open at the time.

- Consider developing a set of common questions to be used in all initial interviews.

- Make on-campus interviews as comprehensive as possible; a school tour, students, faculty peers, and potential supervisors should all be included, but don't forget to give the candidate some downtime.

- Interviewers should discuss interview procedures in advance and be aware of questions and topics that cannot be addressed; do not make assumptions about candidates—read résumés carefully.

- Offer candidates of color or openly LGBT or non-gender-conforming candidates the opportunity to meet with peers.

- Interviewers should return a common feedback form to hiring central.

- Be clear about the process with candidates, and keep them informed about what is happening; each candidate should have a "case worker" to maintain contact and answer questions.

- Be sure to inform candidates of travel reimbursement policies and procedures.

- If asking candidates to teach sample classes, provide enough lead-time and be sure to consider experience level; observers should fill out a common feedback form.

- PERFORM REFERENCE CHECKS! Do not assume anything, and make personal contact with references.

- All offers of employment should be conditional on the results of reference and criminal background checks.

- Perform driving record (if appropriate) and criminal background checks, even if the school's jurisdiction does not require them; consider credential checks, as well.

- Don't rush the process. Be patient and remember the importance of hiring.

- If the school is losing good candidates on a consistent basis, consider conducting interviews with lost or withdrawn candidates; review the results as part of the preparation for hiring process.

- Begin to trumpet the virtues of newly hired teachers as soon as the contracts are signed.

Chapter Five
Induction

Maxim Five: Induction matters.

Some readers may be uncomfortable with the use of a "public school" term as the title of this chapter. The sometime Latin teacher in me, however, likes "induction" for a number of reasons. Like a novice in a religious order or even a newlywed, a faculty member new to our school—even if they are an experienced teacher or has come from another profession—needs to be gently and warmly led into the new culture that will become their professional home. A simple orientation, just pointing the person in the right direction, is not enough. Through a formal and intentional process of induction and an equally formal and structured mentoring process, new teachers can be given the professional competence and confidence that will start them on the path to greatness.

The Teach for America program trains its recruits in the art of teaching for five grueling weeks and still receives enormous criticism for putting students "at risk" because of these new teachers' inexperience. In light of this, it might seem curious that academically respected (and very expensive) independent schools are able to "get away with" hiring untrained teachers. That this system does not spell educational disaster is a tribute to those aspects of independent school culture that have made even the most superficial orientation programs work: relatively small schools and classes, close supervision, common mission, and students and faculty who are motivated toward student success. And even the slightest effort to build upon these factors in the design of a teacher induction program can yield even greater success.

Good induction programs have four components: 1) the identification of new teachers' needs, both individual and general; 2) the development and execution of specific actions that address those needs; 3) communication of questions and expectations, mutually and in many forms; and 4) opportunities for the new teacher to receive feedback.

The "leading in" begins the moment a candidate says yes to an offer of employment. At that instant the relationship changes from a mutual wooing to a professional partnership in which the teacher offers service in return for certain considerations from the school. Crudely, a salary and benefits may seem to make up the bulk of these considerations, but the school is morally and practically obligated to provide a good deal more if the teacher's potential is to be fully realized.

The first thing the teacher needs to be told is what happens next. The school should be able to give the teacher at least a rough timetable of important events before the start of the work year, expectations for work before that time, and the name of key contact people to whom the teacher should turn for answers, advice, and direction. Typically, an important first contact will be whichever business officer handles contractual issues, benefit sign-ups, and the other bureaucratic aspects of becoming an employee of the school. Another contact should be someone who is either in an immediate supervisory or partnership role with the teacher—a department head or a co-teacher, for example. All this information is best conveyed to the new teacher in writing, with appropriate telephone numbers and e-mail addresses included.

At the same time those who will be supervising the new teacher should be taking a few moments to consider and discuss the new teacher's individual needs. Along with textbooks and whatever specific resources will be available to help the teacher plan courses and activities, the question of strengths and weaknesses should be addressed. Where will the new teacher need the most help or guidance—curriculum, subject-matter expertise, classroom management, acculturation to independent school life in general? How can the school best tap the teacher's strengths in a way that will not be overburdening? Some beginning teachers have the confidence to state out front those areas in which they believe they will need help, but it is incumbent on the school to anticipate such needs and to have a plan for addressing them. Whether the new teacher needs actual training or just a series of heads-ups will depend on their experience level and maturity, but no school should forget that many of its ways are likely to be unfamiliar even to a veteran teacher.

Schools can do much to increase the odds that new teachers will have satisfying and successful years by assigning them classes that make sense based on their experience level. To throw a rookie into a required course that other members of the department avoid or to give him or her the section with all the toughest students in the grade is a recipe for frustration or failure. There is no justification—not even "we all had to go through it"—for this kind of trial by fire. A limited number of preparations might be in order. If the school has a strong and active mentoring program, a modestly reduced load in the first term and some clever scheduling allow mentor–new teacher meetings to take place when they are needed most.

A few new teachers will have their contracts in hand even before they have received a college degree. Many of these will be graduating from liberal arts colleges where they have received no formal training in education or child development beyond perhaps an introductory psychology course. They may have tutored, worked at summer camps, or done some sort of community service in a school setting, but their exposure to pedagogy and curriculum design is limited to what they have observed as students. Most are "school smart"—good in class and strategic in their work habits and organizational facility. A few have succeeded by well-hidden acts of narrow escape, and fewer still have been superb, assiduous students who have crossed every T and dotted every I since kindergarten. The latter two categories—breezy, intuitive, often charming but not terribly diligent students and those who cannot understand why every student is not as good or as hard-working as they are—can have the most difficult time adjusting to the rigors and vagaries of classroom and school life. The potential and long-term prognosis may be excellent for them, but the first year is likely to present these young people with a steep learning curve. If they can be identified early on, they can be given the supervision and guidance they need.

Along with individual needs, the school should be developing programs and materials that will familiarize the new teacher with the culture, practices, policies, and values of the school. This is emphatically not simply the work of a single morning before the opening of general faculty meetings, nor is it a matter of mailing out the school handbook a few weeks before school begins. Even the most exhaustive of recruiting materials will not serve. New faculty need to be given attention and information so that they may begin their first day as a teacher, coach, and advisor as fully fledged members of the faculty.

Whether or not a system is in place to use mentors in an ongoing way to guide and support new faculty, there should be someone at the school—possibly someone from each division in a large school—who holds the brief as "director of new teacher services." This person, probably an administrator, becomes the point person for new teacher issues, the person to whom new teachers know they can turn for answers or advice (or at least redirection) and who is responsible for maintaining the schedule of ongoing meetings and training sessions throughout the new teachers' first year, including in-school summer training. The person must be enthusiastic about working with new teachers and possess the wisdom and tact to guide them toward improved performance and a growing sense of their own capability.

Materials provided to new teachers as soon as possible ought to include the school calendar, as much information as possible about the curricula they will be teaching, and access to the school's communication services—telephone, online teaching resources, and e-mail. The time before starting a new job is often a time of personal transition, including moving; a school telephone extension and e-mail address that can be checked remotely can feel like a surrogate home to someone who is living out of boxes or driving cross-country with a rented trailer. Not incidentally, this information also provides a dependable line of communication between the school and the new teacher. An account and password access to such resources as an on-line curriculum map—particularly the data from previous years of courses the new teacher will inherit—and course-management sites would be invaluable. Faculty handbooks and student handbooks are also crucial.

A number of books can be helpful to those embarking on their first year in a classroom. Some, like the classic The First Days of School by Harry and Rosemary Wong or The Skillful Teacher by Jon Saphier and Robert Gower, are comprehensive how-to manuals that are dry but packed with ways for teachers to present themselves, organize classrooms, and conduct teaching activities. Others, like The Students Are Watching by Theodore and Nancy Faust Sizer, approach teaching as a moral, political, or transformative activity. Another classic, "Why are All the Black Kids Sitting Together in the Cafeteria?" and Other Conversations about Race by Beverly Daniel Tatum, sets forth the fundamentals of multicultural understanding in a school context; Gloria Ladson Billings' The Dreamkeepers does much the same, with an even more pedagogical focus. For teachers who will be working with students with a range of learning styles, the All Kinds of Minds organization provides both comprehensive information and an empathetic viewpoint. Whatever the book, whether it is presented as a gift to incoming faculty or is required reading for the induction program, the idea that there is wisdom to be gained from books on teaching and education is an important part of imbuing new teachers with a sense of their part in what is both a profession and an intellectual tradition.

In some cases a school may be able to outsource some training for teachers who are absolute beginners. The school may suggest or require (and pay for) a methods-and-materials or educational psychology course at a teacher-training college, or send new teachers off to one of the growing number of beginning teacher programs offered by regional independent school associations. Schools with a religious affiliation may send new faculty to programs run by the religious body. Along with practical advice on teaching skills, these programs touch on general aspects of professionalism that can give new teachers an idea of what to expect in school and what will be expected of them. Such programs are costly, but they provide a general introduction to the work. Participants leave with a sense of heightened confidence as well as an awareness of issues in teaching that in some cases they had not anticipated. But even the best of these programs cannot substitute for efforts to help new faculty understand your school and what it is like to work there.

Above all, new teachers should be given ample opportunity to discuss their courses with those with whom they will be sharing a class or with a department head or other supervisor. The more questions that can be answered early on, the stronger the teacher, the stronger the program, and the better students' learning experiences will be. Even if the other tenth-grade English teacher is out of the country until the very day general faculty meetings begin, someone needs to make certain that the new teacher has as much information on the curriculum—content, calendar, assessments—as possible. There is no excuse for a new teacher to be hung out to dry on this for an entire summer. It's not acceptable to offer only things like, "Don't worry, it'll all come together when X gets back" or, "We're not really sure whether they actually read *The Bluest Eye* last year. Z didn't leave any of that information behind."

If the new teacher is replacing someone, the school is obliged to see to it that the departing teacher leaves behind sufficient materials, or at the very least makes time available to meet, so that the new teacher is not floundering for lack of direction, content, and even materials as the year begins. Book and equipment orders should be done; if the new teacher has ideas or can be consulted before these are completed, all the better. We all know too many horror stories about teachers new to a school who have arrived in August to find no materials, no existing curriculum, and no one who is in a position to help—or whose e-mails requesting help or get-togethers have gone unanswered. There is no excuse for such behavior.

Schools that are able to provide support for new teachers to meet and plan with their new peers will find the return on even a modest investment such as a small daily stipend to cover such work is considerable. New teachers will be confident in their material, feel supported in their planning, and regard their new workmates as true colleagues. If personal relationships develop through this work, the long-term pay-off in terms of possible retention will be even greater. It is through working together and breaking through the isolation that has marked teaching for too long that commitment to the profession, and to a school, is born. If you have no formal mentoring program, establish a buddy system pairing a new teacher with a veteran at least from late summer through the first few weeks of school. There might even be a small stipend for the buddy or a small social budget to cover a lunch or dinner or two.

Whatever programs the school offers for new faculty (and new non-teaching staff, too, as appropriate) should not be available only to those brand new to the profession. A thorough induction program could last from two days to a week, with a series of sessions offered by school leaders in different areas: school history and culture (try a historical walking tour of the campus); curriculum and assessment ideas commonly used; a sense of the school's academic standards and expectations; norms and initiatives relating to multiculturalism and diversity; terms and lingo with specific indigenous significance (at a school we worked at we distributed a comprehensive—and fun to assemble, with a group of colleagues brainstorming together—vocabulary list); classroom management, discipline, and student-faculty relations; the mentoring program; a comprehensive technology orienta-tion; a library and media services orientation; a walk-through of the school year, featuring highlights, command performances, and "crunch times"; and above all opportunities for new faculty to bond as a cohort and to feel comfortable on the campus and with the ad-ministrators and teacher-leaders who present the sessions. Session format can include case studies, panels (including students), discus-sions, and hands-on projects. Good sessions will model the expectations and techniques of good teaching and collegial behavior in the school. The mood should be light, the dress code relaxed, the food (including break snacks) plentiful and tasty, the venues and present-ers varied and congenial. Session leaders may also want to assign short readings—articles on some aspect of teaching and learning—to be discussed as part of the program. Some time each day could be set aside for teachers to work on curriculum or lesson planning, with the day's session leaders available for individ-ual consultations.

Along with students, where their presence would be useful, it is also important to bring families into the induction process. A be-fore-school event for new faculty is an ex-cellent time to introduce a few parents and guardians—class parents, parent associa-tion officers, representatives of other parent groups—to new faculty. The point is simple: to provide a chance for new faculty to get to know parents (often the *bête noir* of beginning teachers) as friendly people and more importantly for some key parents to gain in-person knowledge of new faculty in anticipation of the second-hand judgments that can sweep the "carpool caucus." A social event with significant others invited will quickly humanize each group for the other; the addition of mentors and a few other administrators and faculty and some thoughtful attention to the demographics of the invited parents will multiply the effect.

A few schools have a new teacher–parent "buddy" arrangement. The value as a form of mutual demystification seems clear, although the school should be cautious not to set up either party as a repository for the unhappiness or as a *de facto* defender of the other. Such arrangements would seem best put in place before the start of school and then let go of soon after.

Internships, apprenticeships, or other formal "teacher training" programs are a somewhat separate issue. For schools that have established such programs as real pre-service/in-service opportunities for aspiring teachers to learn the craft through on-the-job training, the induction process, like the selection of candidates into the program, must be more finely crafted than for typical, full-time, journeyman teachers—even raw recruits. Usually lasting a full year, such programs are built around the trainees' duties in the school as well as a full curriculum of workshops and seminars in aspects of curriculum, pedagogy, and child development (sometimes constituting part or even all of an earned degree). A school that has chosen to put its resources into such a program, occasionally in partnership with a university, is in an enviable position with regard to its ability to build and maintain a professional culture that inspires and rewards teaching at all levels.

By the time general faculty meetings begin, new teachers should already feel as though they are part of the school community. They should be familiar with important parts of the campus, be somewhat versed in the special patois of the school, be able to greet by name a goodly handful of people, and feel a nascent sense of ownership in the courses they will teach. Even in the bewildering buzz of mass introductions, divisional and departmental meetings, and words of wisdom from on high, new faculty should feel as though they are among friends. There will still be plenty to learn and many missteps to make, but they should not feel alone as they maneuver their way through the first few weeks of school.

In the absence of a comprehensive mentoring program, the calendar for a teacher's first year should at the very least include a series of scheduled meetings with administrators or teacher-leaders. These should have two purposes: one, to provide a forum for questions and answers, and two, to go over topics of critical importance, such as how to handle parent meetings or how to write narrative comments. Although some first-year teachers will be shy about asking questions of administrators, once a discussion is started, people often will be quite candid. Obviously, these meetings should not be the only times when teachers can raise issues or seek advice. Peers, department heads, counselors, and other leaders of the school need to go out of their way to make themselves available and be helpful to first-year faculty. A school with a culture of aloofness will have a hard time retaining faculty, and when aloofness, or something that looks like it, is spotted in the new teacher, it requires attention. Often enough a tendency to shy away and isolate oneself masks insecurity that can be assuaged by the helpful intervention of colleagues.

The beginning teacher must of course figure out how to be themself as a teacher. For some the persona that feels right and to which students respond comes naturally, but for others, developing the right balance between an act and a natural self takes agonizing years. The best advice I ever received, as I struggled early in my career to be the teacher I imagined I needed to be—a cross between General Patton and Mr. Chips, as I recall—was to be myself, to let my idiosyncrasies, humor, and vulnerabilities show through, but also to let my students know the things about which I was serious and would expect them to be the same. What I failed to realize then was the value of feedback. Had someone come to my class early on, just to observe and let me know what they saw, I might have been able to learn the lesson about being myself earlier.

Feedback is the magic word here. What beginning teachers crave (although they may not realize it initially) is thoughtful commentary from a supportive (or at least disinterested) observer, someone who can see what is going in the classroom and report back to the teacher.

Robert Burns' pretentious but lousy neighbor in church could not see herself as others saw her, but technology gives us this gift today; teachers can actually watch themselves teach via video recording. Many beginning teacher programs now ask participants to prepare and record a short lesson, which is then critiqued by the teacher and a few peers. Many participants report that this is the most valuable part of such programs, and Steve

Clem, whose "Eloquent Mirrors" workshops on observation and feedback defined these tasks in the independent school world, recommends self-recording and private self-critique as a powerful tool for improving practice. (Steve would wryly suggest a day's wait and a glass of wine before viewing oneself.) Beginning teachers, whether or not they have experienced a program that involves taping, should be freely encouraged, perhaps even required, to record at least portions of a class or two early in the year; the school's technical resources should be directed toward this practice. If recording is out of the question, then a friendly, non-threatening peer—someone who will not later be formally evaluating the teacher—could be asked to observe and offer feedback.

What should the observer (including the teacher, watching a recording in the privacy of their own home) be looking for? The list is long, and it may evolve as the teacher develops the desire or sophistication to look into problematic or interesting patterns in the classroom. The literature on classroom observation is considerable, and there are particular observational techniques and strategies designed to gather specific data. For a beginning teacher, calling patterns, board use, and classroom movement are good starting points; voice modulation and tone are also worth looking at. Just observing the actions of students in the classroom is an education in itself. Feedback from a second party should be given as dispassionately as possible, and the observer might want to start a session debriefing an observation by asking the teacher what they think happened in the class before moving onto a factual re-counting of what was observed and then, if the teacher wants, warm and then cool feedback. Many teachers will find this whole process uncomfortable at first, but some embrace the concept wholeheartedly and their performance improves considerably as a result.

At some point, an administrator will be doing the observing, and any formal observation should be prefaced by a meeting to set a time and ask the teacher about the goals and content of the class and to find out if there is anything in particular they would like the administrator to look at. This sets a tone of helpfulness. After the observation, follow the same process of asking the teacher about their impressions and then recounting what was observed. The administrator can then offer feedback on the observation.

It is important to distinguish between observation (looking at what is happening), feedback (commenting on what was observed), and evaluation (judgments based on what was observed). Although a formal administrative observation is by its nature evaluative, it is the feedback rather than the judgment that will be of most value to a new teacher, and even veterans will need help in adjusting to the standards and expectations of a new school.

It is impossible to overstress the importance of keeping new teachers well informed throughout their first year—and especially not to assume that veteran teachers will always "get" how things are done just because they have done more or less the same things before. Regular check-ins at key points and brief, but mandatory, tutorials on specific skills for all new faculty are the minimum standard in the cultivation of successful teaching that is the goal of any induction program. New faculty need clear, easily accessible resources and opportunities to help them quickly understand and adapt to the culture of the school. It is equally important for the school to be aware of the concerns of new faculty in order to continuously improve the induction program. Above all, there needs to be leadership for this work and a commitment from the school to doing it well in order to sustain faculty professionalism and maintain the high quality of student learning experiences.

Many schools—and a great deal of educational research—have found that, along with institutional commitment, the establishment of a program of direct, personal support for each new teacher is critical to success.

Best Practices
in Induction

- New teachers must be "led in" to the new school's culture, not just "oriented" to it.

- Consider the specific individual needs of newly hired teachers.

- Appoint someone, informally of formally, as "director of new teacher services."

- Establish regular communication with new teachers; provide key contacts— co-teachers, department heads, etc.

- Provide as much material as possible to new teachers; collect curriculum materials from departing teachers; consider maintaining curriculum maps, which can be useful resources in this situation.

- Consider assigning reading to new teachers to introduce them to important aspects of school life, teaching practice, and the teaching profession.

- If a teacher requires specific pre-service training, provide it; consider sending new teachers to regional independent school teacher training/induction programs.

- Design and offer a comprehensive before-school induction program, featuring aspects of the school's academic and non-academic programs as well as its values and culture, and offering opportunities to meet colleagues.

- Develop induction materials based on new teachers' needs: rules, calendar, curriculum, standards, "lingo" unique to the school, emergency procedures, etc.

- Consider supporting before-school curriculum development work in which established teachers work with new ones.

- Assign new teachers course loads and classes based on experience levels and expertise; do not give new teachers the sections or courses that "nobody else wants to teach;" set new teachers up for success.

- Give some families a role in the induction process to humanize new teachers for parents and vice versa.

- Consider the establishment of a full-blown mentoring system, or at least a new teacher-established teacher "buddy" system.

- Set up a program of regular "new teacher check-ins" at important points in the year, and have a curriculum of topics to be covered—parent conferences, comment-writing, etc.

- Provide early and frequent opportunities for new teachers to receive non-evalua-

tive feedback on classroom and other performance—through a mentor, a "buddy,"
or the use of video.

- Consider the establishment of a full-
blown internship/apprenticeship/teach-
er-training program.

Chapter Six
Mentoring

Maxim Six: There is a reason that Mentor shows up early in the Odyssey.

Homer begins the *Odyssey* with the setting forth of the young Telemachus, the son of Odysseus, on a journey of his own to find news of his father. Worried lest his youth and inexperience lead him astray, Athena appears to Telemachus in the guise of the aged Mentor, a sometime companion of Odysseus and something of a sage. Mentor offers the wisdom and advice that the young man needs to make a good start on his quest.

Like Telemachus, each new teacher in your school, no matter what their previous experience, is sailing uncharted waters. I once heard a colleague describe their school as a "minefield" for new teachers, even though on the face of it the school community was close-knit and its atmosphere genial and benign. Until understood, however, the ways and mores of a new school can trip up even the most seasoned of teachers.

Many educators in the Baby Boom generation speak fondly of some older educator who took them under their wing as young men and women and acted as mentors. Many were administrators, and the advice they gave had much to do with finding one's way along the track toward the headships that seemed, particularly in those last days of some of the long-term "giants," the logical career pinnacle to which they should aspire. Not everyone was fortunate enough to have such a mentor, and those who did not sometimes envied those who did.

The unevenness of this sort of informal mentoring system did little to improve the lot of every teacher. It was not until the last few decades that the term has found another, more generalized and programmatic use in independent schools. Beginning in the 1980s, although there may have been some earlier instances, many schools started to assign a faculty partner to each new teacher in the school—someone perhaps older and wiser but certainly more experienced in the particular school—to provide informal guidance to new teachers, answer questions, and act as a sounding board. The degree to which these mentors and their charges (the linguistically impure term mentee evolved to describe them) actually interacted, and the amount of support or advice the mentors actually gave, varied greatly. Schools might have had only the vaguest of ideas as to who was a great mentor and who was not. In addition, personal relationships might or might not develop, adding another significant variable to the mentoring equation.

In recent years, the importance of mentoring programs has become much clearer and research done in the public school sector has suggested that effective mentoring is one of the most significant elements of teacher retention beyond the first year or two. A teacher who has experienced a thorough and thoughtful induction program and is then supported through the first year of teaching by a mentoring system that has real substance is simply more likely to hit the zone of comfort and enthusiasm where good and happy teachers need to be.

A substantial and comprehensive mentoring system has its costs, and to do the thing well a school should be ready to bear these costs in the interest of the future quality of its teaching faculty. In some schools mentors are paid small stipends; in others there is a slight reduction in teaching load. The director of the mentoring program may have a reduced teaching load and there may be expenses related to events or social budgets for mentors. Although there is no hard evidence as to the actual return on this investment in independent school contexts, even the potential reduction of *sturm und drang* as a first-year teacher flounders seems like a worthwhile benefit. Of course, there is no guarantee that a new teacher will follow the advice of a mentor, so there is no ironclad certainty of success. However, the more structured the program, the more easily can its tenets be implemented.

A comprehensive mentoring program could begin with the hiring season itself. A school can solicit volunteers to participate as mentors, and these mentors could even be given a role in the interview process—as tour guides, perhaps, or hosts at lunch. At some schools that have worked to develop a culture of mentorship, the mentor-designate even participates in the selection of the trainees; the relationship may even begin at the interview stage. Under more usual circumstances, though, the person at the school charged with new teacher services would have in mind a pool of potential mentors to be matched with newly hired teachers on a case-by-case basis.

Matching a mentor to a new teacher is more art than science. Good arguments can be made for several courses of action, but on one point there is general agreement: the mentor should in no way be in an evaluative role. As to other factors, gender matching usually makes sense, as does age matching—although many successful mentors are considerably senior to their charges and occasionally vice versa. Whether the mentor should be in the same department or general field remains open to debate—although the mentor should probably be in the same division as the new teacher. If possible, the new teacher and mentor should not share a course; the working out of curriculum involves another sort of relationship. At some schools geographical proximity is a primary consideration; the hope is that the pair will run into each other occasionally throughout the day, making possible consultations on the fly or at least the exchange of friendly greetings. The matching of mentors and new faculty from underrepresented minorities facilitates the exchange of experiences and advice particular to their situation; on the other hand, it is important to avoid isolating or separating minority faculty or creating the impression that diversity/equity/inclusion is owned only by faculty of color. Probably the most important match factors are temperament and interests, and therefore matchmaking should be done thoughtfully.

Above all, mentors should be flexible, generous of spirit, and sufficiently experienced both to give wise counsel and to be able to represent the culture of the school. An effective mentoring relationship will not inevitably evolve into a personal friendship, although many do. The mentor also needs to be able to offer expert professional critique in a positive way; some programs involve extensive training program for mentors in observational techniques and teacher coaching.

Once selected and matched, mentors should be given a clear idea of what is expected of them by way of scheduled events and meetings and they should be given the contact information for their charges. A friendly phone call or e-mail as soon as possible is a nice gesture of welcome to the school community, and the new teacher is likely to have questions. If there are opportunities for summer meetings, even for coffee or lunch, the relationship can be off to a good beginning. If the school is willing to provide a social budget to underwrite such gatherings, so much the better.

The most highly elaborated mentor programs have developed what are essentially curricula to carry the participants through most of a school year. In addition, some schools have created comprehensive new faculty manuals that include specific mentorship meeting times and topics as well as a full program of workshops on upcoming events in the school. Putting these events on the school calendar gives them a significance that ensures they will take place. Ideally, it would be possible to synchronize a free period for the new teacher and mentor, even if only during the first term of the year.

The mentor's actual work will change as the year progresses. They will be sometimes a consultant, sometimes a confessor, sometimes a tutor. What matters is that the mentor and the new teacher have time to meet, and that this time is as sacred as a scheduled meeting in a school can be. Even if the relationship is strictly on a professional level and no personal chemistry has begun to develop, it is important that the pair meet at least to review upcoming events and discuss any issues that may have arisen.

Successful mentoring programs tend to involve a component of observation and coaching. To be done well, the mentor should receive some training and guidance in effective observation techniques and on the art of "reading back" what is observed and giving feedback—up to and including the making of judgments and suggestions. Here it is essential that the temperament of the mentor be suited to this delicate and sometimes difficult task. Mentors can also learn specific techniques for coaching teachers on classroom management, building positive and productive classroom culture, and developing an effective and authentic classroom persona.

If the school has developed a mentoring curriculum and scheduled times for workshops to take place, these should mirror and anticipate the school calendar as much as possible.

If parent conferences loom, then the workshop topic should be about conducting conferences and the art of communicating messages of concern. If the end of the term is near, the new faculty should be hearing about ways of anticipating and managing the time crunch that will suddenly make completing every task on time seem impossible. The composition of narrative reports is a specialized art in any school. It is impossible to give new teachers too much guidance in completing these. Otherwise, the mentoring curriculum should address major areas of the teacher's skill set. Basic to these should be classroom management, curriculum design and using assessment effectively. Also on the agenda: effective activity leading or coaching; equity and multiculturalism in the classroom and the community; developing positive relationships with colleagues of all ages and backgrounds; and maintaining effective and appropriate relationships with students and the nature of professionalism as it applies to independent school teaching. Teachers new to the profession, especially, seem to need and appreciate ideas about how to maintain a balance between one's job and personal life. There should be discussion of worth ethic and the fact that effective teaching involves giving more of oneself uncomplainingly than is asked of one's peers in many other walks of life. It is better to introduce the subject preemptively than to make it the topic of a lecture after a problem has arisen.

In many schools the mentoring season is concentrated in the autumn, although some partners find themselves in a much more sustained relationship. The scheduling or regular mentor–new teacher meetings into and through the winter offers the possibility of building even richer relationships—and the mentor may be a useful ally the first time a new teacher experiences the midwinter doldrums.

How a mentoring program is organized and how much time, humanpower, and money the school wishes to devote to a real program for first-year teachers will depend very much on its situation and perceived needs. Some schools with strong and highly collegial cultures have relied for years on informal relationships that develop in the course of things and that seem to bring new teachers along naturally; generous teachers of wide experience and with a commitment to the success of new recruits find ways of making the first years of teaching a rewarding experience.

But if we see teaching as a craft that can be learned and commit ourselves to making true professionals out of the new teachers who come to our schools, the need for structured and well-managed programs is clear. If nothing else, a school should provide new teachers and their mentors with a basic script addressing topics specific to the school and general issues related to teaching, learning, and professionalism; this script should be keyed to the school calendar where necessary. Mentors should be asked, if not required, to observe new teachers' classes and to offer feedback and guidance. The mentor's classroom or office should be a "safe space" for new teachers to vent frustration or ask the most basic of questions. The mentor should embody the school's optimism for the new teacher and be able to represent the school's support—and, if needed, tough love. This is a tall order for those who are chosen to be mentors, and it is a powerful act of faith for a school to develop a comprehensive mentor program.

There is another benefit to building a strong mentoring program. Research suggests that teachers who act as mentors represent a potential cadre of school leaders—teachers who care about the profession and have been active participants and facilitators in a formal program to improve the quality of teaching as well as the quality of life for colleagues. The cultivation and recognition of good mentors, like the cultivation of beginning teachers, creates another tool with which journeyman and master teachers can hone their craft and take pride in their participation in the advancement of the profession. A successful mentor should consider their work a résumé-worthy, and schools at the recruiting stage should be on the lookout for veterans of first-rate mentoring programs.

Each year's new faculty will bring surprises: new folks of spectacular ability, some who need a great deal of attention, and perhaps a few of whom the school may be tempted to despair. In the Foreword to this book I boldly asserted that good teachers could be made. Much of the curriculum of a comprehensive mentoring program is based on the skills, content, and habits of mind that are the essential ingredients of good teaching.

Best Practices in Mentoring

- Establish and be prepared to fund a comprehensive mentoring program.

- Appoint someone to manage the mentoring program.

- Establish a pool of flexible, knowledgeable, and enthusiastic mentors; mentors should be committed to the success of new teachers.

- Mentors should not be in supervisory or evaluative roles vis-à-vis new teachers; mentors sharing courses with new teachers can create difficult situations.

- Train mentors in techniques of observation, sharing feedback, and teacher coaching.

- Set and maintain a calendar of mentor-new teacher meeting times.

- Develop a mentoring curriculum and materials to support it; include such topics as maintaining a balance between work and personal life, collegiality, and work ethic.

- The mentor should offer a "safe space" for the new teacher and an ally in solving problems.

- Regard trained and active mentors as a cadre of potential teacher-leaders in other areas.

Chapter Seven
Training Teachers

Maxim Seven: Good teachers can be made.

If you are of the persuasion that teaching is a genetic or even magical endowment, I hope you will concede that the skills of even the most gifted natural teacher can be sharpened. But don't worry. In this chapter, I will not propose some lock-step method for turning out teachers like Model T Fords. I believe there are a few underlying characteristics shared by all good—and great—teachers: They want to teach and they believe that teaching is worthy and satisfying work. Above all, they believe in students.

What should a good teacher be? In what areas of teaching performance should a teacher be strong? Using a functionalist approach, I have appropriated and then tweaked the basic categories of evaluation that we developed at a school where I worked for many years, based on a document we created a number of years ago titled "Effective Teaching at Our School." While I do not pretend that we are the *ne plus ultra* of effective schools or that our evaluation system is an ideal to which every school should aspire, the collective intelligence of an admirable faculty has gone into the development of this list. I am confident that it covers, in a general way, essential aspects of good teaching that apply in all independent schools.

The effective teacher:

- is an expert and passionate participant in their subject area

- maintains a disciplined and productive classroom

- maintains a classroom in which individual student learning needs and capacities are honored

- sets clear and appropriately challenging academic standards and expectations for all students

- plans and executes substantive curriculum and assessments

- provides timely and appropriate feedback to students

- is committed to helping students understand content from multiple perspectives

- maintains a collaborative classroom learning environment

- applies technology appropriately as a tool for teaching and learning

- is punctual about deadlines and obligations
- is effective in the role of advisor and mentor to students
- is effective as a leader of sports and student activities
- is committed to expanding their own knowledge and practice of teaching and child development
- actively supports and promotes diversity and equity in the curriculum and in the school community
- actively supports and enforces the rules and policies of the school
- communicates effectively and appropriately with families
- actively supports the mission and values of the school through professional behavior

I believe strongly that effective professional development in all forms, coupled with a supportive and positive school culture and the individual teacher's own will to learn, can make *anyone* a good teacher. Some of the qualities listed, it is true, must be exhorted and cannot exactly be taught as skills—punctuality, for example—but they are no less achievable for that.

Let's look at what each of these qualities looks like, how it can be taught or even
inspired, and how it can be observed and
strengthened.

**The effective teacher is an expert and
passionate participant in their subject
area.**

Of course, any teacher hired has at least
a fundamental mastery of the subject matter
they are to teach; this can be observed from
a résumé or a college transcript. But having
had a college major in Chemistry or Early
Childhood Education is only a start. All
fields, including languages and English literature, are in a constant state of evolution
in the academy, and related pedagogy is also
changing. The literary canon expands and
changes, and I have heard the assertion that
the sum of scientific knowledge doubles about
every eleven years. New evidence brings about
new understandings of historical events, and
our knowledge of the way students learn continues to expand.

It is not too much to ask that teachers at
all stages of their careers make an effort to
keep current in their fields. This may mean
doing outside reading of books, magazines,
and academic journals or belonging to professional organizations and reading the on-line
materials they publish for K–12 educators.

Teachers should be excited about what they teach; anecdotal evidence suggests that memorably effective teachers express an undisguised passion—even to the point of obsession—for their subjects.

Schools can support these passions by making it an expectation that each teacher will belong, at the school's expense, to at least one subject-matter-related professional organization and receive its publications. Department or division meetings could feature regular reports from faculty members about topics they found interesting in these materials. The support given to faculty continuing education courses—including the earning of advanced degrees—may vary by school, but any school that asks a faculty member to teach in an unfamiliar field should go to extraordinary lengths to ensure the teacher's expertise before the class begins. Even a series of tutorial meetings with a nearby university professor would be worthwhile.

As part of the professional development program, faculty should be asked each year to complete a brief résumé update relating to recent work or reading in subject matter areas. Some teachers go well beyond this, writing for professional journals relating to their fields, publishing their own fiction or poetry, or presenting at conferences; many fine arts faculty regularly show or perform their work. In these ways teachers can demonstrate their expertise and passion—and of course such passion will be readily observable to any student or classroom visitor.

The good teacher maintains a disciplined and productive classroom.

For many teachers, particularly those at the beginning of their careers, classroom management, a.k.a. discipline, is the greatest challenge of all. The difficult classroom is a source of pain and embarrassment to the teacher, of frustration and irritation to the school, and of sometimes-vehement anger to parents and guardians. Most importantly, children do not learn well in a classroom in which disorder reigns and in which the teacher does not command respect.

We all know what the unruly and unproductive class looks (and sounds) like. An evolved system of mentoring, featuring classroom observation as one of its elements, can be extremely helpful to a teacher struggling to maintain order in class. Alternatively, early administrative observations and thoughtful feedback and proactive suggestions can provide the sort of early action that beginning teachers, especially, need. There are specific observational techniques— the teacher can be encouraged to video and view the class, perhaps several times—and a whole repertory of specific actions that teachers can take to establish a classroom culture based on mutual respect.

There may be times when stronger action is needed. A learning specialist or school counselor could observe the classroom dynamic, or, in rare instances, a class will require a pep talk (or sermon) from an administrator enlisting the better angels of the students' natures. In instances where the situation is dire, the teacher may grow so frustrated and insecure that counseling is needed; at worst this is the onset of the loss of faith and self-confidence that can spell the end of someone's desire to teach. Early intervention is critical to forestall the collapse of the teacher and the loss of learning that can occur when issues of management and discipline become destructive. A situation involving a chaotic classroom and a desperate teacher should not persist past mid-year.

Not all noisy or apparently disorderly classrooms are unproductive, however. There are teachers at all grade levels who seem to be able to work in an atmosphere that drives squeamish observers batty, yet where authentic, active learning takes place in the hearts and minds of excited and even inspired children. The school and the teacher will have to come to a mutual agreement as to a tolerable level of chaos, but the noisy yet productive classroom is one of the glorious complexities with which schools must learn to live.

The effective teacher maintains a classroom in which individual student learning needs and capacities are honored.

Of all the things that can be taught to teachers, skills and sensitivities relating to learning styles and cultural needs and styles are among the most straightforward. Frequently, the problem is simply for teachers to understand that there is great individual variation in the ways students learn and that this variation can be both neurological and cultural in origin; the apparently lazy or inattentive or extremely quiet student is that way for a reason, and they can be taught if that reason is understood.

There is some debate over the nature and even the existence of "learning styles," but classroom techniques can be learned through reading and professional development that will enable teachers to "reach" students with a variety of preferences and strengths without having to go through contortions of unitary differentiation, at least in a typical independent school classroom. Many of the techniques that work well for students with specific learning weaknesses also work well for other students. Experience will bring teachers quickly to an understanding that students do come with "all kinds of minds," and that an alert, trained teacher can teach those minds well.

It is important, not to say ethical, that the school be honest about the specific learning needs of individual students. A school that does not reveal to teachers the existence and nature of pre-existing student testing or learning profiles does a serious disservice to students and teachers alike.

Cultural differences in learning are not about capacity but rather about attitudes toward learning and the roles of the teacher and the student. In cultures in which collaboration or humility are considered cardinal virtues, for example, speaking up too often in class or racing to put one's hand in the air are considered unseemly. Students brought up in these traditions are often underestimated or even disparaged for their reticence in American classrooms. In some traditions teachers are expected to act in a directly authoritative role, and the failure of an American teacher in a constructivist classroom to be a stern authority figure is seen as weakness and as a failure to show proper respect to students. Much research has been done on gender in learning, although there is still considerable debate as to what the real differences are in how boys and girls best learn. The work of Lisa Delpit (*Other People's Children*) and

Gloria Ladson Billings (*The Dreamkeepers*) specifically address cultural differences in the approach to learning, and all educators should be familiar with the work of researchers like Carol Gilligan (*In a Different Voice*) and Lisa Damour (*Untangled* and *Under Pressure*) on girls' learning.

A teacher's capabilities in this area can be observed by noting classroom interactions and calling patterns, by looking at projects and other assessments for variations that will measure the learning of students with different ways of thinking and learning, and perhaps by looking at patterns in grades and comments—does the range of grades include pockets of students who share particular learning styles or cultural backgrounds? The latter is sometimes difficult to see in the small sample provide by only a few classes, and in any case it is the teacher who should be encouraged to do the looking. Anecdotally, the matter is simpler: Do all students in the teacher's class feel a level of success commensurate with their honest effort?

The effective teacher maintains high and clear standards and expectations for all students.

Effective teachers expect only the best from their students, and they knows how to encourage students to produce it through a combination of toughness, encouragement, and specific advice. A truism about memorable teachers is that they are recollected as having been "tough"—invested in student success but unwilling to compromise their standards or accept work they believed was below the student's capabilities. Student always knew where they stood with these legends.

On an institutional level, teachers can be taught a sense of what good or excellent work is through a process of consultation with peers and supervisors. Although exercises in group grading can be frustrating as a method for establishing meaningful common standards, they can be useful in helping teachers understand such basic things as what the school or department values as categories of performance and generally what the gradations of work, poor to excellent, look like. It is fundamental that a part of any induction program be spent explaining whatever marking system the school uses, as well.

On an individual level, teachers communicate their standards and expectations to students in many ways—through the work they assign, through their words of correction or praise, through other non-verbal cues, and of course through the way in which they evaluate student work. Students learn quickly what a particular teacher will accept and what will pass as satisfactory performance and behavior in their class, and so they require consistency from each teacher. They also need to know that each teacher cares about them personally and is invested in their success, and that the evaluation the teacher gives to a piece of their work is not an evaluation of *them*. Teachers need to learn to talk about a student's work dispassionately, as a problem to be solved rather than simply a problem; the attitude of the helpful editor is more effective than the attitude of the irritated pedant. These skills should be taught within the division or department, by example. Here, especially, the teacher's belief in the capability of every child is essential; the attitudes of colleagues can do much to reinforce this belief.

Teachers can help themselves communicate standards for work by the use of evaluation rubrics that set forth the categories being evaluated and the criteria for each level of performance. There are many resources for teaching the design and effective use of rubrics, and they can take many forms, from simple scoring guides to elaborate grids filled with specific descriptions of work of a certain quality. A useful exercise involves asking students to participate in the design of the rubrics by eliciting their ideas of what truly great work on a particular project or assignment would look like—they know very well, and they can help the teacher produce a detailed and useful document that will show exactly what the standards are and how a student can achieve at the highest level.

Whether a teacher is maintaining high standards and expectations can easily be observed by looking at materials they create and by sampling evaluated student work. Are the standards clear? Does the work seem appropriately extensive and challenging for the ability level of the students? Is the teacher using consistent language when asking for certain types of student performance? Grading patterns can also be of some use in gaining a sense of a teacher's standards.

The effective teacher plans and executes substantive curriculum and assessments.

In the last four decades there has been a quiet revolution in curriculum and assessment. The textbook is no longer regarded as the curriculum but rather as one among many resources, and the teacher is no longer the center of the class. Several similar curriculum models and theories have taken leading roles in the way that effective teaching happens. Constructivist teaching, based on the neurologically sound idea that students "construct" understanding based on a combination of prior knowledge and carefully shaped learning experiences, has meant a diminished role for rote memorization and an increasing number of project-based and experiential learning models.

Theodore Sizer's work with the Coalition of Essential Schools produced the concept of "teacher as coach"—the "guide on the side" instead of the "sage on the stage." The Teaching for Understanding model, developed by David Perkins and others at Harvard's Project Zero, and the similar Understanding by Design model, developed by former independent school teacher Grant Wiggins and his colleague Jay McTighe, base curriculum design on "planning backwards." In these models, design begins with the establishment of content and understanding goals and then builds forward toward learning experiences that will lead students toward demonstrable achievement of those goals, as shown by precisely designed assessments. "Authentic assessment" puts a premium on asking students to solve complex, "real world" problems. A variety of methods, from traditional quizzes to elaborate projects, can be used to assess how well students with many kinds of learning styles are mastering material and on what areas students (and the teacher) need to be working harder.

No longer does the weekly trudge through a textbook chapter, followed by a test, constitute the sum of all planned learning experiences. Even several less "progressive" curriculum theories, notably Direct Instruction and E.D. Hirsch's Core Knowledge, have been well elaborated as effective curriculum. Workshops and other professional development resources in all these methodologies are readily available, and good teachers—and good schools—ought to make an effort to become familiar some of them.

Whether a teacher is designing and executing substantive curriculum should be readily apparent by an examination of the curriculum materials—assignments, resources, assessments—that the teacher is using in class. Along with examples of other aspects of the teacher's paper "work product"—copies of evaluated student work, course documents, written comments to students—these materials should become part of a file or portfolio of that documents the teacher's practice and growth.

The effective teacher provides timely and appropriate feedback to students.

The notorious Skinner Box is a simple but sophisticated device for assessing learning in laboratory animals. The learning takes place when the creature performs an action and then receives feedback—food for correct performance, no food for incorrect. The teaching is actually done by the animal itself within the designed experience, but the learning can be quite complex. The key to the learning is feedback.

In most school contexts, feedback is some sort of evaluation of learning—a grade, a star at the top of a paper, a "good job" or "not quite" comment in a class discussion. It can also be the teacher or coach's manner or even body language; even scolding someone in the lunch line is feedback. Feedback is essential to student learning; it tells the student how they stand relative to the standard. The best kind of feedback is both immediate and loaded with information as to how performance or standing can be improved.

The teacher who sits on a growing pile of papers for two months, immobilized at the prospect of grading them all, is failing their students in many important ways. Students without any sense of how they are doing has no way of improving their performance, and in the absence of specific suggestions, there can be no change. The teacher is also sending a message that they do not care very much about their students or their learning, that other things are more important than honoring their work by attending to it in a professional way.

In every school there are teachers who are slow—some famously so—in returning student work. Some pull this off by laying claim to a kind of intellectualism against which little things like grades do not matter. Others may be just lazy, and there are those—and I have been among them—who avoid the task of passing judgment on work completed in good faith, knowing that in students' eyes we are in some way passing judgment on them.

Teachers need to be monitored in this respect. Unfortunately, the best source of information on laggard teachers is usually students, who are often more patient than they should be. Periodic grade book checks for very new teachers could be useful, but the fact is that this can be a difficult situation, fraught with defensiveness and excuses.

Changing bad behavior is a challenge. Perhaps the most effective technique is an ultimatum, supported by regular check-ins. Perhaps a couple of slow graders could make a pact for mutual support and aid, or an efficient worker could take the slower one in hand. Many teachers find that the use of rubrics makes the grading process speedier; the clear criteria and categories for evaluation facilitate at least some of the decision-making. Occasionally it turns out that the culprit simply assigns far too many pieces of work for anyone to grade and return; discussions of curriculum can root out this particular problem.

A school policy on returning work is one way to address this issue on a global level, but it will not catch everyone. Address the problem through vigilance, exhortation, and support where it can be provided.

The effective teacher is committed to helping students understand content from multiple perspectives.

Helping teachers develop their capacity to teach students to see the world through multiple perspectives is largely a matter of helping them develop their skills at project and activity design, devising assessments that require understanding a multiplicity of points of view. For teachers schooled in the old ways, finding a zone of comfort with ambiguity can be a challenge, as can the need to step away from textbook certainties. In this area, teachers will benefit from being deeply involved in their fields on a professional level, where multiple approaches and even controversies are more common.

Teachers at all levels should be familiar with Benjamin Bloom's Taxonomy of Educational Objectives in the Cognitive Domain. The taxonomy is a hierarchy of levels of understanding and mastery; at the higher levels come analysis, synthesis, and evaluation, all higher-order thinking skills that are associated with the ability to see issues from many angles. Most of the versions of Bloom's Taxonomy available online and elsewhere include suggestions as to how teachers can frame questions and tasks so as to elicit cognitive response—thinking—at a particular level. This can be a powerful tool for helping students widen their horizons.

A check of lesson plans and observation of classroom activities will give evidence of a teacher's work in this area, another argument for the development of teacher portfolios.

The effective teacher maintains a collaborative classroom learning environment.

This is a multi-layered category. On one level, it addresses the simple question, Do people get along? On another, it goes to the matter of sharing values around working and learning. On the more observable but also more complex level, the category speaks to the way in which the teacher organizes learning experiences and tasks. Does a student plow through the teacher's program alone, maintaining a parallel course with every other student, or is the classroom a place of interaction, of projects that ask students to cooperate and share their efforts and ideas?

"Cooperative learning" was all the buzz a generation or so ago, and the idea remains with us that students learn well when working cooperatively in groups. The fabled Harkness Table discussion format is enjoying broad exposure of late, and some of the more elaborate techniques for organizing classroom discussion—Socratic Seminars, fishbowls, jigsaws, and even hevruta paired learning— are effective ways to let students articulate and rehearse ideas and understandings and to raise the learning level of the entire group. The kinds of ensemble work typically found in performing arts classes can be adapted to other kinds of classrooms, and putting students in small groups to master (and then perhaps present to classmates) skills or content—much as coaches use small groups to hone particular sports skills—can bring great results. Teachers can learn these techniques either through books or workshops and experiment with different ideas until they find those that are comfortable and effective. In the end, any technique that asks students to listen to one another, to articulate their thoughts at a high level, and to consider and reflect on what they have heard, is a collaborative learning tool.

Large-scale collaborative projects, either long- or short-term, require careful design if they are to be successful. The profession of project management provides a number of useful ideas for organizing groups, assigning sub-tasks and interim deadlines, and then assessing the performance of group members. Any major project requires elaborate planning and careful monitoring on the teacher's part;

failure to do this well almost inevitably means a failed project. Even if good-quality work is turned in the failure is in the equity of effort and learning of the group members.

Evidence of a collaborative learning environment can be observed through classroom activities and lesson plans as well as in documentary evidence in the teacher's project and assignment file.

The effective teacher is able to apply technology appropriately as a tool for teaching and learning.

This may be the most practical aspect of good teaching. The degree to which a teacher elects to include technology in their teaching is largely a matter of individual knowledge and preference, but ideally the use of technology should be a matter of informed choice. Most schools now expect a degree of teacher proficiency in basic productivity tools—word processing, e-mail, perhaps spreadsheets and presentation software. Many teachers are more than comfortable using and teaching with software tools specifically designed for education or relating directly to their field.

Technology is a fact of life in schools and more importantly in our students' lives, and to pretend it is not there is foolishness. Whether a teacher is a techno-deity or merely a home eBay user, what matters is that they recognize the importance of technology in students' lives and understands that educational work can be done with great efficiency using a range of technologies. The good teacher knows that technology is only a tool for teaching and not an end in itself. The good teacher has been given the opportunity to learn how to use that tool and knows when to use it, or not.

Effective professional development programs in technology focus on the articulated needs of teachers. Schools with vital technology programs continually look for ways in which specific undertakings can be enhanced by technology. The technology staff may "scout" good resources and then bring suggestions to teachers, but in the end the technology "solutions" must work for the teacher in the classroom. Teachers lagging in key skills can be brought along through individualized programs; using off-site resources can be very effective.

Classroom observation, lesson plans, and assignment sheets will show how much and how effectively a teacher is using technology. Be aware of over-use: too many PowerPoint shows, too many films (the DVD player as "electronic babysitter"), too many hours with classes doing Internet "research," too many student projects involving videos, are tricks and gimmicks that may be standing in for substantive teaching.

An effective teacher is punctual about deadlines and obligations.

Nothing is so undermining of faculty collegiality than having a few teachers who are consistently late to or frequently absent from obligations. Nothing is so annoying as having a few colleagues who are always late with paperwork. A school in which meetings always start 10 or 15 minutes late has allowed corrosion to set in. For one thing, the habitual lateness or absence of others gets under the skin of those who work hard to be on time and present. For another, the students are watching.

The only solution is for supervisors to call people on their behavior and to make clear that lateness in whatever form is unacceptable. If tardiness is endemic to the community, the demand for change must start at the top—even if the top is part of the problem. The same holds true for those during-the-day absences. Checking e-mail is not an excuse for missing morning assembly or the first half of lunch. The culprits are known, if not to you then to the administrative staff or department-mates or co-teachers who have to cover for them. Confront them, and demand improvement. And model good performance.

The effective teacher is effective in the role of advisor and mentor to students.

This category addresses the ability of the teacher to work well with students in non-academic, one-on-one situations. Some teachers are naturally good at this—wise about problem solving, about boundaries, about transferring initiative to the student when necessary. Some teachers work easily with some types of children and not so easily with others.

Good teachers have learned a few strategies for connecting with students that work in most cases, and have been instructed about establishing appropriate professional boundaries. Whether being an advisor is a formal part of the job or arises *de facto*, good teachers understand that their first responsibility is the child's best interests and safety. They respect the role of parents and guardians. They have been told the school's policies on confidentiality and the notion of risk. They know when to promise to keep a secret (essentially, ***never!***) and when not to. Their training has included some case studies and role-plays as well as a review of child and adolescent psychology. They know when to call for help or when to direct a child to someone an expert.

Effective advising and mentoring is easy to see. Students interact naturally with good teachers and seek them out as needed—and sometimes more often. These teachers are in regular contact with counselors or administrators, sharing stories and information and asking for advice. They may have groupies, but the group is neither exclusive nor absurdly large, and its membership changes; the group does not hide itself as a "secret club" or cult.

Ongoing professional development, beginning at induction, is the key. The teacher does not have to be King Solomon, or Sigmund Freud—in fact, the self-styled therapist is a danger and must not be allowed to practice. The teacher need only be reminded regularly of the principles of good advising and of the school's particular policies. If they are doing an effective job, the results will be apparent in relationships with students and, often, in the lack of anxiety transmitted to administrators by their families. Although crises are mercifully few and far between for most advisors, effective ones will immediately seek help. There will be plenty of conversations and consultations as the matter is resolved, because, more than anything else, the effective advisor and mentor is concerned about their charges.

Many evaluation systems ignore this part of a teacher's work or give it very short shrift. A brief description of what effective advising looks like, either as a rubric or as part of the standards for evaluation, can be very helpful not only in judging quality but also as a basis for conversations for those deemed in need of further training.

The effective teacher is effective as a leader of sports and student activities.

Like the effective advisor, the good teacher-coach or activity leader or advisor puts the best interests of their charges ahead of all other considerations, including win–loss records and Model United Nations trophies. Students involved in their activities or teams are excited, happy, and confident, knowing that they are developing the skills they need and developing a positive group bond even if they are 0-and-10.

The first order of business for helping the good teacher be more effective in this area is to give them a clear sense of the school's philosophy and goals. Does winning matter more than participation? Are the school's clubs expected to work on a semi-professional level, or are the students just supposed to be enjoying themselves? The answers to these questions are essential if the teacher is to understand and fulfill this role.

The professional development of coaches is, in most quarters, woefully neglected. Although the science of sports coaching and training has advanced by light years in recent decades, school coaches are still too often thrown out onto the field with little more than a bag of balls, a whistle, and a rulebook. The clinics that town and regional team coaches regularly attend often go unnoticed by independent school athletic directors, and only injury-prevention, rule-change clinics, or league meetings are deemed worthy of attendance. A few coaches—varsity level—may be obsessive enough to take themselves to clinics or summer coaching camps, but on the whole sub-varsity coaches are expected to operate on their own memories as players, on whatever tips they can garner from peers, and on instinct. It is perhaps no wonder that few schools include coaching as part of an overall evaluation program.

A further issue comes with the increasing reliance on out-of-school coaches. While they may have the expertise and focused enthusiasm for the sports that schools like, they often lack knowledge of the school's culture and values as well as the professional knowledge about child development and effective—and psychologically safe—mentoring that teachers receive through the school's induction and professional development programs. Any effort to connect outside coaches with the school's culture and values will make them more effective in their work with students without impinging on their win–loss potential.

In the area of activities, finding the resources to train teachers is admittedly more difficult. I have watched brand-new teachers flounder with newspapers, yearbooks, Odyssey of the Mind teams, and many other student activities. Advice from previous, failed holders of the same titles was not helpful, nor was the advice offered by administrators or other veteran colleagues. In retrospect, activities of this magnitude should be placed in experienced hands, with newer teachers in apprenticeship roles. Whatever good ideas can be gleaned from nearby schools or yearbook companies, the Private School Journalism Association, or other entities associated with these endeavors can only help.

As I noted earlier, coaching and activity-leading seldom appear as categories in evaluation programs, although they may make up a significant portion of a teacher's job description. A school that has systematized observation, feedback channels, and standards for effective work in these areas will have no problem recognizing and continuing to develop good teachers.

The effective teacher is committed to expanding their own knowledge and practice of teaching and child development.

I have been throwing around "professional development" as a comprehensive term to cover myriad activities, all directed toward

improving the professional https://www.adl.
org/education-and-resources/resources-for-ed-
ucators-parents-familiescompetencies of
teachers. Much professional development
should be unavoidable: induction, mentoring, and whatever programs occur in an "all-
school" context. Regular refreshers in child
development and the psychology of learning
should be a part of the experience of the whole
faculty. The good teacher expects this kind of
professional development and embraces it as
a matter of course.

But for some teachers, particularly of
the old school, professional development is
anathema. It may be that they have been
through too many administrators' enthusi-
asms of the moment and have seen too many
fads come and go. They may have had to sit
through mind-numbing all-day workshops
by experts who lectured on student-centered
learning or practiced "trust falls" with colleagues they barely knew and trusted less.
They may be classroom stars—brilliant, intuitive, even unorthodox. But when professional
development looms, they schedule root canals.

The good teacher, whether required to do
so or not, sets goals related to being a better
teacher and then seeks the resources to achieve
them. They look for opportunities to learn
more about teaching, about subject area, and
about the minds and hearts of students. This

teacher is the one bugging the academic dean about the conference on brain-based learning or filling out the application for the National Endowment for the Humanities summer programs. This teacher becomes involved in projects at the school on curriculum development or advancement or campus planning because they are interested in learning more about schools and teaching.

The teacher's annual résumé update gives plenty of evidence about commitment to expanding their repertoire. Perhaps the teacher has been able to publish a paper or article on teaching or present at a professional conference—in terms of building teacher confidence as well as reflecting some light on the school, the best professional development there is. The good teacher who hungers for more knowledge will be easy to spot in each year's opening meetings: they are all ears.

The effective teacher actively supports and promotes diversity and equity in the curriculum and in the school community.

Statistically, the chances are pretty good that the teacher is white and grew up in a predominantly English-speaking, heterosexual, and materially comfortable environment. And yet the teacher finds themself in a school environment in which terms like multiculturalism, equity pedagogy, white privilege, and social justice are bandied about every day.

Even in schools that remain majority white, diversity matters in immeasurable ways. Class, sexual orientation, gender expression, religion, and other less visible differences abound. Independent schools share a commitment to building strong multicultural learning communities, and to do this they require the informed and heartfelt commitment of teachers, administrators, families, and students. The good teacher takes it upon themself to become informed, to understand the nature of unearned privilege and the nature of racism in our society. They want to become a strong and active ally of others in the school and in the world who seek to effect change, and above all they want to bring these understandings, and the understanding and appreciation of other cultures and ways of being, into the classroom.

In every corner of North America there are experts in diversity and anti-bias work who will train faculties in the language and action of multicultural learning and equity pedagogy. NAIS can provide resource suggestions and support to schools on every kind of diversity initiative. Faculties can form study groups around particular texts or join the National S.E.E.D. Project, a program of the Wellesley (College) Centers for Women begun by Peggy

McIntosh, author of the famed monograph, "White Privilege: Unpacking the Invisible Knapsack," first published in NAIS's Independent School magazine. Many local advocacy groups maintain educational offices, and national organizations such as Facing History and Ourselves, the Anti-Defamation League, Teaching Tolerance, and Primary Source can provide support for curriculum development around multicultural themes. The good teacher's school will have no problem finding high quality and academically credible resources to use.

Within the school, there may be opportunities to step forward as a member of a diversity or multicultural committee or to pilot curricula on equity or social justice themes. The goal is to place the ideas underlying this work in the hands of students so that they may go forth and change the world.

The effective teacher actively supports and enforces the rules and policies of the school.

As intentional communities, schools have developed rules and policies that support their missions and their fundamental values. A teacher who signs on with a school has implicitly pledged to support that mission and those values, and on the level of rules and policies, the teacher is obligated to do the right thing.

It is the school's responsibility to make clear the nature of the rules and their enforcement to all members of the community.

The good teacher, although there may be school rules and policies with which they do not personally agree, makes an effort to be vigilant and to make certain that students understand the rules and do not break them. The teacher does not turn a blind eye to infractions nor collude with students or colleagues in selectively ignoring misbehavior or the abrogation of school policies.

That said, a teacher should avoid being seen as a martinet, so rigid about rule-breaking as to cast an anxious pall on campus. The happy medium is a dispassionate (never angry!) kind of enforcement that takes the form of a dialogue where possible and a scolding only when the offense is severe: "I see this behavior, which I believe is against our rules; I am obliged to enforce this rule by telling you to stop and (if the offense warrants it) by punishing you. Do you understand why I am doing this?"

The good teacher uses words of sharp remonstrance or disappointment sparingly, and resists the temptation to "go nuclear" and lose their temper in a histrionic display of righteous anger. Disproportionate anger is the teacher's worst enemy, and self-righteous or exceptionally volatile teachers must learn to master their feelings if their enforcement is to be seen as fair and just by students, who know and are adept at provoking a hot temper when they see one.

A school's system of rules and discipline must be simple, clear to all, and above consistently applied. New teachers are often reluctant to confront minor misbehavior because they do not wish to risk their good relationships with students, while some veteran teachers choose to quietly ignore issues they do not believe are worth the struggle. The administration must regularly remind faculty and model for them the need to speak up when a rebuke or reminder is needed. The administration must be scrupulous in its efforts to apply the same standard of behavior to all members of the community, but also to dole out administrative sanctions with clarity and proportion.

A number of schools have subscribed to programmatic systems relating to student behavior. Usually based on the development of skills for communicating emotion, these programs, like Open Circle and Responsive Classroom, tend to be geared toward the elementary and middle grades, and they provide developmentally appropriate themes and even scripts for helping students learn to treat others, and themselves, with respect. These programs also offer extensive teacher training and resources.

Other discipline models range from "one rule" schools, honor code schools, and schools with complex bodies of rules and sanctions. Whatever the case may be, a thorough explanation of how the system works should be part of training at induction, and all teachers should be observed relative to their participation in enforcement efforts and reminded to do the proper thing if need be.

A teacher who has serious disagreements with a school's rules and policies has three choices: to leave the school; to go along with the rules; or to work within the system to effect change. Not a few school leaders have risen from the ranks via campaigns to change a school policy. Sadly, teachers who opt to leave as a matter of "conscience" seldom do so for that reason alone, and they often go away mad.

The effective teacher communicates effectively and appropriately with families.

While in the not so distant past communication with parents and guardians was largely the province of day school teachers and boarding school administrators, the culture of all independent schools has been transformed by technology to require that teachers be in regular contact with families. At the high school level, this contact tends primarily to involve advisors, but frequently circumstances—concern about a student's performance, a minor disciplinary situation—mean that a teacher must call or e-mail a family with bad news. For many teachers this responsibility is the very worst part of the job. To deliver an unwelcome message about a child to a parent or guardian who is frequently older and, in their protective role, at least a little unpredictable can be a formidable task. Many teachers dodge it altogether.

Primary and middle school cultures tend to involve more regular contact to keep parents informed as to both ups and downs. This can become burdensome as some families' expectations grow to the point that the household wants regular briefings from the teacher, over and above scheduled conferences and narrative reports.

The issues are two: having teachers understand what their basic responsibilities are and making certain that necessary communication is taking place. Some schools have a rule of thumb, or even just a rule, that teachers must call families in specific circumstances—a poor term grade looming, a major test or project bombed, a certain amount of work missing, demerits or their equivalent given. A school would be wise to similarly recommend that teachers contact families with good news under specific circumstances; if parents do not like surprises of a negative sort, they love positive ones. Almost all schools have policies regarding response to parent-initiated contact via e-mail or telephone—expecting a response within 24 hours is common.

Whether, how, and when teachers make those calls is a larger issue. Preparation, guidance, and record keeping are the keys. The parent/guardian relations portion of a mentoring curriculum should involve role-playing a potentially difficult telephone conversation along with face-to-face conference preparation. Some teachers prefer to squeeze in calls during free moments in the school day—necessitating contacting the parent or guardian at work—while others resign themselves to a couple of evening hours each week on the telephone. Many teachers wisely will not leave messages on home answering machines lest they cause hurt student feelings or are intercepted and deleted by the student. All calls should be logged and noted for future reference or in the worst case as part of a paper trail regarding a student problem.

If the school can provide guidance and support, and if teachers can be confident that the school will stand behind them in all areas of family relations, they will be in regular and appropriate contact with families. This will mean sharing good news and bad and in doing so acknowledging the family's role as partners in the child's education. Parents/guardians seldom express concern about teachers who keep them informed. Good teachers understand this aspect of the job and, no matter how difficult it may seem at times, do it well.

The effective teacher actively supports the mission and values of the school through professional behavior.

What exactly is "professional behavior"? It is abiding by the rules of the school as stated in published policy guides, abiding by the law, and observing a few commonsense rules of behavior for teachers—generally geared to limiting social excesses and modulating the public expression of political or spiritual views. And it is knowing how to conduct one's life appropriately within the school community.

Schools should be clear in their personnel policies about what is unacceptable behavior or what may constitute grounds for termination "for cause." Model policies can be found, but these describe situations that are clear-cut at least in relation to the idea of professional behavior. The trickier realm of professional behavior includes issues of confidentiality and discretion. A teacher is entitled to their opinions about a student or a colleague, but in most situations, short of actual risk to the child, these opinions are better left unvoiced. A teacher may believe that a school is moving in the wrong direction, but where and when to make that belief known is a matter of professional judgment. Taking one's grievances to a Board member may seem like a way to strike a blow, but the grievance had better be substantial and real, and the use of the Board a last resort. Moving so far outside commonly acknowledged channels of governance can be perilous and potentially damaging to the teacher as well as the school.

But how does the effective teacher know these things? They might seem to be common sense, but if the topics are never raised, a teacher coming from far outside the independent school tradition or the world of service to children may not be aware of them. They are not "crimes," and they are seldom "cause." They are simply bad manners and bad strategy that can reflect badly on the teacher and the school. Teachers should be told this.

Easier areas to deal with involve the world of unstated expectations. What is the faculty dress code, really? What social events are truly command performances? Are teachers expected to attend every game, play, and concert? If a teacher does not drink, are they still welcome at the Friday happy hour gathering? Are significant others invited to the faculty–Board dinner if the invitation does not specify? Is it safe to bring a same-sex partner to an event that includes parents and guardians? If nothing else, there should be someone to whom new teachers should be directed for "official" answers to questions like these at the beginning of their term of service—someone frank, knowledgeable, and above all discreet. As time goes by, the answer person may become the school's Emily Post, a valuable role.

The good teacher will acquire a sense of what professional behavior is by listening, by asking questions, and by consulting their own sense of propriety. The observable aspect will be crystal clear on both the positive and negative side.

One overall aspect of teacher training that cannot be overlooked is the importance of administrative modeling. What school leaders want teachers to do—participate, grow, be punctual—they must do themselves. The school's executive leadership must be seen to be enacting the ideals that they hold up for the faculty at large in order to establish a culture in which teachers will aspire to and achieve the highest levels of professionalism and efficacy.

Effective teachers can be made. A school devoted to helping each teacher function at the highest level and feel successful in all areas of professional life will instill in its faculty

a sense of the importance of their work and
the immense value of doing it well—of being,
above all things, good teachers.

Best Practices
in Training Teachers

- Establish the school's standards or criteria for effective teaching as the basis for teacher training, professional development, and evaluation.

- Ensure teachers' subject-matter expertise and enthusiasm. To do this:
  - Hire experts when you can, provide training when you cannot
  - Track teachers' involvement in subject-area through portfolio or regular résumé updates
  - Make subject-area professional development available whenever possible
  - Support faculty membership in and participation in subject-area professional organizations and activities

- Support teachers in maintaining productive, orderly classrooms. To do this:
  - Use observation and feedback
  - Identify in-school and outside resources to train or remediate teachers in this area
  - Have clear lines of authority and support for teachers in difficulty

- Focus interventions on positive change and, where necessary, on students

- Know when apparent disorder is in fact productive excitement; understand individual teacher differences

- Ensure teachers' knowledge of individual student needs, capacities, and styles—cognitive and cultural. To do this:

  - Train teachers to recognize and respond to different learning styles and, where necessary, learning disabilities; be sure that teachers understand the emotional aspects of learning difficulties

  - Be clear and open with teachers about the needs of the individual students they teach

  - Train teachers in equity pedagogy and cultural aspects of student learning

  - Train teachers to understand how gender, race, and ethnicity can affect student learning and attitudes toward education

- Support teachers in setting and maintaining high standards and expectations. To do this:

- Be certain that all teachers care deeply about the success of each student
- Share ideas and approaches; make standards a regular topic of teacher conversation and meetings
- Observe teachers at work; look at lesson plans, texts, classroom activities, samples of evaluated student work, and teacher-created materials for evidence of clear and appropriate standards
- Encourage the use of rubrics as a tool for communicating standards to students and for providing meaningful, standards-based feedback on student work
- Support teachers in developing expertise in curriculum and assessment. To do this:
  - Provide training to teachers in specific, appropriate methodologies relating to curriculum and assessment design: Understanding by Design, Teaching for Understanding, constructivist theory, project- and problem-based learning; teachers should be aware of the theoretical and practical frameworks upon which such ideas are based

- Create a professional culture in which a textbook does not equal a curriculum

- Encourage teachers to use a variety of assessment techniques and strategies to measure student learning

- Observe teachers at work; look at lesson plans, texts, classroom activities, assignments, and teacher-created materials for evidence of thoughtful and effective design

- Support teachers in providing students with meaningful and timely feedback. To do this:

  - Observe teachers at work; look at assessments, classes or activities, and samples of evaluated student work for evidence of clear, immediate, comprehensible, and meaningful feedback on student performance

  - Be alert to teachers who are slow in providing feedback; set standards and establish supports; establish ultimata where necessary

  - Encourage teachers to use rubrics both to streamline the evaluation process and to provide clear feedback

- Support teachers in helping students see material from multiple perspectives. To do this:
    - Encourage teachers to keep up-to-date in their fields in order to understand the complexities current of
    - Train teachers in the design of projects and activities that promote multiple-perspective understanding
    - Train teachers in the use of Bloom's Taxonomy as a tool for designing curriculum that asks for understanding on various levels, including analysis, synthesis, and evaluation
    - Observe teachers at work; look at lesson plans, texts, classroom activities, projects, and teacher-created materials for evidence that multiple perspectives and approaches are being acknowledged
- Support teachers in establishing collaborative classrooms. To do this:
    - Train teachers in collaborative, cooperative, and interactive classroom techniques: jigsaws and fishbowls, Socratic Seminars, debate formats, Harkness Table seminars, "teacher as coach" methodologies

- Train teachers in the design of effective collaborative projects and in the evaluation of student performance on collaborative work

- Observe teachers at work; look at lesson plans, classroom activities, projects, and teacher-created materials for evidence of collaborative and cooperative learning

- Support teachers in the use of technology as a tool for teaching and learning. To do this:

  - Train teachers in all technology whose use is required by the school

  - Make specific, tailored training in other technologies available on an individualized, as-needed basis

  - If the use of a new technology is mandated, support and encourage stragglers

  - As a school, be alert to but circumspect about reports from "early adopters" and "scouts" as to promising technologies

  - Observe teachers to make certain that they do not rely too much on technology at the expense of other kinds of teaching

- Ensure that teachers are punctual and present. To do this:
  - Model punctuality and appropriate attendance at the administrative level
  - Observe teachers to make certain that they are punctual in meeting obligations
  - Address unpunctual behavior and set specific expectations where necessary
- Support teachers in developing their skills as advisors and mentors to students. To do this:
  - Train teachers about the role of an advisor in the school
  - Train teachers about policies and good practice relating to advising: boundaries, ethical and legal obligations, maintaining healthy teacher-student relationships, confidentiality, at-risk behavior
  - Observe teachers in their role of advisors and provide feedback and suggestion as necessary; do not enable ineffective or questionable advisory behavior

- Support teachers in developing their skills as coaches and activity leaders and supervisors. To do this:
  - Articulate and train teachers and teacher-coaches in the school's for sports and activity programs
  - Find ways to train out-of-school coaches in the culture and values of the school as well as the philosophy, goals, and expectations of the athletic program
  - Train coaches in the techniques of particular sports and in team management; look for outside resources (clinics, courses, camps) to raise the level of coaching expertise
  - Do not assign new teachers to lead the most important or largest-scale activities unless they have appropriate support
  - Observe teachers; encourage, recognize, and reward teachers' growth and expanded capacity in these areas; reassign ineffective coaches or activity leaders
- Ensure teachers' expertise in the fields of pedagogy and child development. To do this:

- Make professional development in these areas central to the school's culture
- Consider making professional programs in pedagogy and child development a recurring feature in the institutional professional development program
- Observe teachers; encourage, recognize, and reward teachers' growth and expanded capacity in these areas

- Support faculty in expanding capacity in the areas of diversity and multiculturalism. To do this:
  - Provide anti-bias training for all faculty, staff, and trustees
  - Build faculty professional capacity around such concepts as being an ally and white privilege
  - Identify outside resources that can help the school and its faculty practice equity and multiculturalism
  - Create opportunities for teachers to act on their own interests and preferences in building community capacity around diversity and multiculturalism

- Encourage the development of curriculum and content that supports multiculturalism and a diversity of viewpoint
- Observe teachers; encourage, recognize, and reward teachers' growth and expanded capacity in these areas

- Ensure that teachers support and enforce the rules and policies of the school. To do this:
  - Make certain that teachers understand the school as an "intentional community" based on specific values
  - Make sure the values, rules, and policies of the school are known and clear to all faculty
  - Model consistent support and enforcement at the administrative level
  - Train teachers in the techniques of correction and discipline
  - Consider implementing established behavioral and social programs: Open Circle, Responsive Classroom
  - Allow for the possibility that rules and policies may change and evolve through an orderly process

- Consistency, consistency, consistency
- Support faculty in working and communicating with families. To do this:
  - Develop a culture in which faculty see parents and guardians as partners, and vice versa
  - Clarify expectations for faculty about communication with families: under what circumstances, how often, and when; remind teachers that parents want to hear good news as well as bad
  - Track teacher-parent communication; address problematic situations immediately
- Ensure that faculty support the school through professional behavior. To do this:
  - Clarify the nature of "professional behavior" through case studies or other educational methods
  - Clarify the role and responsibilities of teachers vis-à-vis support of the school
  - Clarify for faculty the appropriate channels of communication for expressing concerns

- Make "professional behavior" a topic of an induction, "buddy," or mentoring program
- Identify someone in the school as the confidential "point person" for questions of procedure and etiquette (What do I wear? Am I supposed to attend? What about my partner?)
- Model desired behavior and attitudes at the leadership level.

Chapter Eight
School Culture

*Maxim Eight: School
culture is everything.*

Thus far I have proposed a long list of
things schools must do in order to recruit,
hire, and train the very best teachers. The
purpose of all this work, however, is not just
to create a corps of stunningly effective, empathetic, and wise educators. It also is to create
a school culture in which the work of teaching
and the profession of teacher are seen as
valuable in and of themselves, as sources of
pride and personal fulfillment on a par with
the pride a surgeon feels on completing difficult, life-saving surgery or the pride of an
attorney who saves an innocent client from
certain conviction. Teaching's relatively low
pay and low prestige in our society make this
a tall order, perhaps, but a school that can
create this culture will not only find it easy to
recruit teachers but also to keep them.

Business publishing in the last decades
has generated a small but interesting genre of
books suggesting that money is not always or
only what fuels the best and brightest minds
in the entrepreneurial world or what creates

corporations that seem to vibrate with energy. Being part of an idea, in particular an idea that attends to the needs and imaginations of people, is as important as the profit motive. The currency by which the value of your contributions to an organization is measured is not only dollars but also the emotional satisfaction of having had the opportunity to contribute. People want to participate and be recognized as part of a successful enterprise, an enterprise with substance and integrity. As Jon R. Katzenbach has written in a book of more or less the same title, pride matters more than money. (But money matters, too, as we will see in Chapter Ten.)

Also in recent years there has been a great deal of writing, in and out of the independent school community, on the subject of school culture and the nature of teaching environments. From Roland Barth to Sara Lawrence-Lightfoot to Susan J. Rosenholtz, authors have considered how schools support and empower teachers in building and sustaining their expertise and commitment. In general what these authors have to say is no surprise: a school that nourishes its teachers, or "furthers" them as the late professional development guru David Mallery might have said, acknowledges their professionalism at every turn. It is also marked by several other characteristics—civility, integrity, and a respect bordering on love. Schools retain teachers by honoring the work they do even as they treat all members of the community with decency, honesty, and humanity.

The creation of a truly professional culture involves directing the programmatic energy and resources of the school toward the development of all the characteristics of the good teacher detailed in the previous chapter. But that is only part of the task. It is even more crucial to build among faculty and students alike respect for, and even excitement about, the idea that excellent teaching and learning are worthy of time and attention even beyond the conventional needs of getting the job done. Aspects of teaching that require extensive institutional commitment in order to build a strong professional culture include professional development, the organization and use of time (the hardest of all to manage), and faculty evaluation.

The development of a thoroughgoing professional development program begins with the assumption that the continuing growth of the faculty in all areas related to the performance of their jobs is essential to the maintenance of an excellent and effective school: academics, athletics, the arts, and student life. A faculty given the impetus and resources to explore new ways of working and new ideas about the work will soar professionally.

We have already established what the content of a comprehensive program of professional development would look like, including opportunities for growth in subject area expertise, classroom technique, curriculum design, the understanding of children as developing learners and cultural beings, and capacity in other areas of student activity.

A superb program must identify institutional as well as personal needs in all these areas and then target resources on the individuals and areas where they will do the most good. For example, institutional strategic priorities or goals may suggest particular areas of curriculum or community in need of specific kinds of development. To support professional development in these areas the school will need to focus on the full faculty, arranging professional days on or off campus or other kinds of workshops that expose the faculty as a whole to ideas or projects on which the school must work. Professional development must and can support institutional development.

If, on the other hand, several teachers wish to become more expert in some aspect of teaching in their discipline or at their grade level, then specific resources should be found to support this effort by sending them to a workshop or bringing in an expert to work with them, perhaps over the summer in stipend-supported work or at a mini-retreat held off campus for a day, afternoon, or an evening. When a single teacher is seen as struggling with a specific skill, whatever help can be given must be brought to bear. Flexible, responsive development is the key, fitting the resource to the need as precisely as possible.

Of course, there are costs to this kind of program, and the obvious ones—workshop fees, honoraria for speakers, travel costs— are only the beginning. The program needs to be planned and managed, which takes time and personnel. If the school determines that the costs of creature comforts—food, lodging, space—are worth a bit of expenditure to achieve specific goals, the price gets higher. Summer work stipends, travel grant programs, out-of-town conference attendance, and other ancillary professional development can be expensive, but when well planned and well monitored, they can be great learning opportunities for teachers and provide great benefits to the school.

Whether a program is budgeted and monitored on a per faculty member basis or as a particular percentage of the operating budget (typically between one and three percent), the school must make certain that teachers are able to participate in the growth experiences that both they and the school need. Some schools leave much of the design of the program in the hands of teachers by establishing individual annual "draw" accounts for professional development, in some cases allowing these funds to accumulate for a set number of years; this provides teacher autonomy, although it may not always answer institutional needs. Most schools fund professional development out of operating revenue, and some are fortunate enough to have restricted endowment available. Many independent schools are eligible for Federal Title II funds, which can offset significant portions of a professional development budget but must be directed to specific expenses.

A handful of schools have made efforts to underwrite some professional development for their own faculties either by establishing professional development centers as part of the school or by offering summer workshops on campus as both a service and a revenue-producing activity. Such programs range from modest—a few brief June workshops in specific areas—or extensive—true summer programs for teachers from around the globe. Such programs can often achieve a number of things simultaneously: provide training for the school's own teachers; give the school's teachers the chance to "show" themselves and their ideas as workshop creators and presenters; and establish the school as a good citizen of the educational community, willing to share its resources (even for a modest fee). Some schools offer themselves as sites for workshops or conferences run by third parties, collecting a site fee, basking in the reflected glory of the program, and securing deep discounts for their own faculties.

A professional development center usually focuses on a few areas directly connected with the school's mission or strategic goals. If presentations or workshops from major figures are offered, it can become a "center of excellence," enhancing the school's standing as a place that takes teaching seriously. It can also be a training ground for members of the school's own faculty who wish to take on the road a presentation about a particular program or idea they have developed.

A school must maintain a collection of professional development resources. These may be part of the main school library collection or a branch looked after by a particular administrator, but the professional development library should include books and other media related to curriculum or pedagogy. It should also hold subscriptions to key publications such as Educational Leadership, Phi Delta Kappan, and Independent School. The Association for Supervision and Curriculum Development offers a number of professional development "modules" on various topics and intended for audiences ranging in size from the single teacher to study groups to entire faculties. Whoever maintains this library might also choose several listservs to which the school as a whole might subscribe, with postings given a special folder or site on the school e-mail system.

High-ticket items like support for graduate study and sabbatical programs constitute a challenge for schools with limited resources. What matters in determining whether such programs are "worth it" for the school are relative factors: Are many thousands of dollars spent on one person going to deliver greater value than that same money spread out over a greater number of teachers? If funding allows these programs to coexist with more broad-based professional development work, the question is irrelevant.

There are ways to fund some of these opportunities so as to reduce costs to the school. For example, graduate work can be funded through a stepped payback scheme, reimbursing the teacher or covering student loan payments only after the degree is earned. This, rather than out-front funding, reduces annual costs to the school and also increases the chances that the teacher will remain to offer several years of service. In some Canadian school systems, teachers take regular "sabbaticals" by working for four years at 80 percent of contract pay and then taking a fifth year as a sabbatical at the same rate; many teachers can benefit from "refreshment" under this system, although the school needs to maintain an enlarged staff. There are creative solutions for every problem, and NAIS and One Schoolhouse, for example, can guide schools wishing to expand professional support for teachers.

The management of time is in many ways the most challenging aspect of building a culture of professionalism. The allocation of time for professional days, in-service afternoons, and departmental or divisional retreats puts professional development in competition with instructional, general meeting, or even vacation time. Someone, or some group, has to determine priorities. If a teacher wishes to do off-campus professional development or if a department wants to take a retreat day to plan a major curriculum shift or to consider grading policies, how are their classes covered? In most schools coverage is provided by peers or administrators, stretching thin individuals who already have full-time jobs. Some schools use teaching interns to cover the classes of absent teachers, and some engage a "full-time substitute," although this system breaks down when multiple absences occur. A few schools contract with substitute providers, either through a local public school system, a consortium of independent schools, or even using one of the several large commercial temporary employment services that have begun to serve independent schools.

Equally important is the matter of meeting time for teachers, and especially time for teachers to collaborate in the development of programs. There is no simple solution to the problem of time for teacher collaboration that does not involve either the expenditure of large quantities of money to expand staffing or the lengthening of the teaching day or the school year. And yet, a school wishing to build a culture of professionalism must find ways to achieve this, either through creative scheduling or through the establishment of protected, even sacrosanct, times for groups of teachers—departments, grade-teams, teachers sharing a course, teachers with a common interest or a project—to meet. Furthermore, learning to talk to one another about teaching—craft, and practice, and technique, and ideas—is a skill that teachers find difficult. There are techniques—the protocols of Looking At Student Work, for example—that can help faculties learn the art of professional communication, an art that the traditional isolation of teachers in their classrooms and the silent one-up-manship sometimes practiced in schools has discouraged.

I have alluded to aspects of a program that would monitor and support teachers in their daily work and in their professional growth by providing feedback and evaluation. There are myriad models of evaluation systems. The most useful of these share several important characteristics: they are geared toward the teacher's professional growth and not toward finding problems; they address all aspects of a teacher's work, including coaching, advising, and dormitory and activity supervision; they are not based solely on one or two unannounced and context-free classroom observations; and they engage the teacher in describing and improving his or her own practice.

From "360" programs that are based on a comprehensive compilation of data on the teacher's work from multiple perspectives (including that of students, in some cases) to portfolio- or peer-based programs, the best evaluations are those that take the viewpoint that the teacher needs feedback—including the positive!—in order to do better work. Most involve work with the teacher even before the start of the year in setting professional goals and determining a course of action that will help achieve them. Classroom observations in sophisticated systems are made using specific techniques that focus on observation, not the making of judgments. Even if the observer may not like what they see, the task is to put opinions aside and attend to gathering data for later discussion and analysis. Pre-observation conferences with the teacher allow him or her to explain the goals of the class and perhaps even request that the observer focus on a particular aspect of the classroom dynamic, while post-observation debriefings can address the teacher's issues as well as discussing the observer's response. The teacher and the observer should be acting as partners in the interest of improving the learning experiences of students, not adversaries in a game of "Gotcha!" in which the administrator-observer holds all the power. This does not mean that a negative or even terminal evaluation cannot be made, but it does means that such an evaluation will be based on objectively developed data.

In the past decade "Folio," developed at the McDonogh School, has evolved into both a comprehensive program that permits the tracking of an evaluation cycle (often a stumbling block for schools) and encourages extensive conversation as the basis for professional growth and also a community of schools, the Folio Collaborative, committed to developing and sharing best practices aimed at faculty improvement.

The nature of a school's methods of evaluation and the attitudes that underlie it can say volumes about the school's culture of civility and integrity. A school where an evaluation system barely exists and is applied only as a weapon to be used against a teacher about whom "rumor says" there are problems or where evaluation is carried out only in the most superficial and random way is sending a negative message about the importance of process and the importance of people.

A school in which back-door deals, in-crowds and out-crowds, and secret plans abound or are rumored to abound, is in trouble. There is little reason for teachers to hang on at such a school—especially those who find themselves left out of the planning or ignored when opportunity and recognition are doled out. There is no magic bullet for turning a se-cretive or toxic culture around other than to eschew secrecy, suspicion, and favoritism and to be conscious of the ways in which human interactions, including the uneven application of policies, can destroy community.

A school should act with consistency, and one of the uses of a mission statement or a statement of values is as a touchstone against which the morality and integrity—in the sense both of honesty and of wholeness—of its actions can be judged. The office of the head of school, in particular, must be a place of trans-parent moral clarity and its actions the em-bodiment of the school's mission. At times this is an unsustainable burden for today's senior administrators, caught up as they can be in ad-vancement and financial responsibilities, but moral leadership must flow from somewhere.

In a school whose culture is healthy, open, and positive, moral leadership may seem to be in the air, and the faculty, like the students and everyone else, is happy to be a part of the community and the culture. And the faculty will want to remain there.

A school can show respect for its members in any number of ways. Wherever people display a spirit of good humor and high expectations, including the expectations students have for teachers and teachers have for one another, there is respect. Where acts of kindness, recognition (but not of invidious comparison), and gratitude abound, there is affection. There are teachers who take pride simply in being a part of a prestigious school, in associating themselves with its majesty, but there are many more who feel what can only be described as love for a school that has shown them, and that shows everyone else, that it cares about them and their work.

It needs to be said that one of the challenges a school faces has to do with romantic or familial relationships between staff members. While some schools have enunciated policies relating to staff dating or to the hiring of multiple family members, most schools take these matters as they come. Many, especially boarding schools, have long and happy histories of teacher couples not only in dormitories but also in other situations, including supervisor–subordinate relationships. Other schools actively avoid such situations, either by practice or by policy; there is no best approach, although it is prudent to avoid situations in which family members are supervising or evaluating one another. Difficulty can arise when faculty members become romantically involved, a potentially corrosive situation made worse when either of those involved is married and most terrible of all when the children of either or both attend the school. Perfect discretion is almost impossible to achieve in a school community, and the side taking, recrimination, active disapproval, and—the worst that can happen—student awareness of the relationship can do serious and lasting damage to the most positive school culture. Here again there is no one preferred practice, although certain behaviors can be cause for immediate dismissal or at least end-of-year termination. It is critical that the school's leadership not be seen as actively taking sides or as meting out unequal penalties; the side the school must be on is that of the students and of its own stability.

Recovery from a destructive faculty "affair" can take time, and the course of action the school must take is to move forward, to remain aware of lasting repercussions—broken friendships, intradepartmental rancor—and to deal with these as best it can. A school that can hold onto its positive values and its ideals will heal all the more quickly.

The challenges a school faces involve the thousands of decisions and actions by its administrators and teachers *each day*, every one of which has, along with its strictly educational intent, an emotional and moral component. There are risks and rewards in each of these actions and decisions, but a school should aspire to an interpersonal culture of respect, integrity, and civility within a professional culture based on confidence in the growing skills of its faculty and in that faculty's excitement about the work it does. A school that can combine these essential positive elements will have little trouble attracting faculty and no trouble at all holding onto the very best of them.

Best Practices
in Creating Strong Professional Culture

- Develop at least a modest familiarity with the literature on institutional culture from the business and education sectors.

- Implement a responsive and comprehensive professional development program that focuses on developing both professional expertise and leadership capacity in the faculty. To do this:
  - Designate a single person or body to manage the program and to develop and allocate resources; remove barriers to access to professional development and build a culture of support
  - Consider institutional as well as individual needs in program design and development
  - Fund the program as generously as possible; make possible such things as retreats, summer stipends, and substitute teachers
  - In particular, support teachers who wish to publish or present their own work in the professional community

- Look for sources of funding beyond operating expenses: grants, restricted gifts, and federal Title II funds

- Consider the establishment of a professional development center or a summer professional development program as a way of spreading the costs of professional development among other schools and as a way of bringing attention to the school

- Establish a professional development library of books, publications, and other materials relating to teaching and learning

- Consider the costs and benefits to the school of travel or study grant programs, sabbaticals of various sizes and purposes, and support for graduate study; if feasible and worthwhile, investigate ways to fund such programs

- Make time available for teachers to develop a true culture of professionalism around issues of teaching, learning, and school policy

- Make professional days, retreats, stipended summer work, and release-time for program development standard practice

- Develop ways for groups of teachers to meet in various configurations to talk about teaching and learning

- Use such techniques as the protocols of Looking At Student Work to build teachers' capacity to talk about students and learning in a focused, productive way

- Develop a growth-focused system of professional evaluation that is consistently applied, comprehensive in its view of the teacher, and keyed to the school's articulated standards for effective teaching; consider becoming a part of the Folio Collaborative.

- Do not enable poor performance or ineffective work by failing to address it when it is observed or reported.

- Be alert to ways in which the appearance or reality of favoritism can undercut the development of a positive school culture for teachers; reward meritorious or exemplary teacher performance in even-handed ways, and respond in the same way to poor performance or malfeasance.

- Be alert to the ways in which secrecy and its nasty complement, rumor, can undercut the development of a positive school culture for teachers; make decisions in as transparent and timely a way as possible; address rumors immediately and truthfully.

- There should be a center or moral clarity in the school; the closer that center is to the office of the head, the better.

- Be alert to the potentially damaging effects of nepotism or romantic entanglements involving faculty; act swiftly to forestall or limit negative consequences.

Chapter Nine
Leadership

Maxim Nine: Not everyone
wants an office.

When I entered the teaching profession nearly fifty years ago, anyone starting out who gave any thought at all to spending a career in independent schools saw a headship somewhere in the future. The Vietnam War may have been raging and countercultural values in the ascendancy, but leading a school, perhaps a school of one's own founding, seemed like the best possible way for an ambitious young educator, a person with ideas, to leave a mark on the profession. The average age of newly appointed heads was dropping in the 1970s, and it seemed altogether possible to join their ranks in due time. Moreover, for many schools then, and not a few now, the number of heads that rose from the ranks of the faculty was a point of great pride.

Over the course of a working lifetime I have had plenty of opportunity to ponder this ambition. On the whole, I have enjoyed being a classroom teacher too much to let go altogether, and yet I flirted with low-level administration as a department head for a number of years before I succumbed to the offer of an office and the opportunity to do for a living what I had long been doing as chair of an active and influential committee. Nowadays I find myself spending far more time in meetings than in contact with students, and I have found that in general the challenges of my position are as interesting and rewarding as teaching students.

There is no denying that the gentle pressure on teachers to consider administrative work has historically been at least slightly more acute for males. Our society has not yet moved completely beyond an expectation that men will automatically aspire to the highest positions available and that a man of talent and vision is obligated to do so. Even so, talented women in the world of teaching also feel the external push to think bigger, and so the question becomes, Must every good teacher become an administrator?

Ever since the "Peter Principle" was expounded in the mid-1960s, most people have been aware that individuals who are well suited for one kind of work in an organization may not be so good at another. The difference between the work of a classroom teacher and that of a division head or a head of school is fairly dramatic, although many similarities can be drawn. The annals of education are filled with stories of those whose temperaments or propensities were superb in the classroom and less than stellar in an office, but the inverse is often true, as well. For some, the differing workload and types of responsibility and accountability are either a bad fit or unsupportable.

A school with a fine and energetic faculty will have to consider questions of ambition and leadership. Some great teachers will inevitably look toward the challenges and rewards of administrative work. Some will look or even make a feint in that direction and then draw back toward the security of the known. A few will be content to teach, serving on committees as needed but generally focusing on their work in the classroom and, as often as not, on personal interests and commitments that exert a stronger pull than a title. There will be a handful, a small one if the school has attended well to its faculty's needs, who will, for whatever reason, fade as forces in the classroom and as positive presences in the school community.

A dynamic school with a vibrant professional culture will not lack for ways to occupy the minds of teachers. If the world of curriculum, practice, and policy is based on a "continuous improvement" model, there will be standing and ad hoc committees, grade-level teams, and study groups in more or less constant motion: reviewing, planning, considering. The spirit of volunteerism will be abroad in the land, and there will be no shortage of chances for even the greenest teacher to participate in the work of the school beyond classroom teaching. A sage administration will parcel out these chances generously even as it works to channel people's energies toward those places where their strengths will allow them to make the greatest contributions.

Most of the qualities of an effective school leader can be found in a good teacher. The leader must know their area, and must be a good listener. They must be optimistic about the people and plans they work with, and must be a flexible thinker and planner, able to collaborate with others and to elicit their best ideas and work. Like a teacher, a school leader must know where they are going—although we call this quality "vision" in a leader. I like to think that vision is not only a fluffy white cloud of possibility or a Grand Plan, although these are important, but also a literal ability to "see the field."

The path from teacher to senior administrator has several way stations, the first what might be called "teacher-leader" and the next, middle manager. The teacher-leader is the teacher whose specific interest or personal qualities draw him or her toward a committee membership or another role in the school that allows scope for ideas and dreams and opinions, now brought forth in an institutional context. Faculty members on Board committees, standing committee chairs, or the "go-to" members of an *ad hoc* team or task force are all teacher-leaders. A teacher-leader can even be "without portfolio," a senior faculty member with wisdom, experience, and a broadly institutional perspective. Often those who fill the role of teacher-leader are volunteers who come to the work through following a particular interest and then become deeply engaged. A school's need for teacher-leaders is bottomless, and the school should do as much as possible to accommodate those who seek opportunity within the school; the secret "tapping" of favored teachers is to be avoided, although there is no harm in issuing invitations to likely prospects.

Middle management includes the department head or "titled" individual whose primary responsibility is in direct student service but who also has some sort of deliberative or supervisory role. Class advisors, "head coaches" with program-level responsibility beyond the team the coach, and dormitory heads fit this description, as well. This administrative level involves greater challenges, responsibilities, and accountability than the teacher-leader role, and may involve a degree of specific training. It is also likely to involve a need for some experience and a thorough grounding in the culture, rules, and policies of the school and of educational practice in general.

Advancement to middle management is often seen as the first step toward advancement to a higher position, and the increased prestige and sometimes pay associated with positions at this level can foster keen competition. A school looking to fill a middle management position—or any other administrative post, for that matter—needs to consider the scope of the search it wishes to conduct and the intensity of the recruiting effort it is willing to undertake.

Some schools make a habit of recruiting for middle management positions from within. There may be a "natural" internal candidate who would be a front-runner even in a national search, or it may just be that the school chooses to limit the extent of its recruiting process for practical reasons. In these schools an experienced and high-performing member of the faculty can at some point begin to anticipate the possibility of increased responsibility in a new position. Difficulty can arise when several people with similar qualifications and experience are plausible candidates; at this point the school might decide to open the search beyond the school or even limit the search to external candidates. There are a few schools that rotate certain middle management jobs, in particular department chairs, on a regular basis. This practice is commendable insofar as it gives significant leadership responsibility to great numbers of people over the years, although these schools must develop mechanisms for maintaining program consistency as leadership roles change.

Other schools make a practice or even a policy of avoiding the political hazards of internal competition for promotion by almost always hiring from outside, even stipulating that internal candidates will not be considered in some searches. A potential internal candidate may be displeased by this practice, but hiring out does bring new blood and new ideas into the school.

There is no one best practice for the recruitment of more senior administrators. The point of a search is to find the person best suited to the position. Whether an internal candidate is hired from an inside track or whether a national search produces a pleasant surprise, the school must serve its best interests. Hard feelings may linger when a popular internal candidate has been passed over—a factor that should at least be considered.

Although retaining the best faculty is the topic of this book, sometimes the larger field of education itself needs to be considered. There will be great teachers, teacher-leaders, and middle managers for whom, in the end, there is no logical next step within your school. Hard as it may be, a school that is conscientious in the development of its faculty may from time to time have to let go of a fine teacher. To hold a talented individual back from pursuing interests and ambitions beyond the school is to deny the human spirit; a school's leadership needs to be wise enough in its career counseling to be able to actively support an individual's growth even if it means losing him or her. In the end, the field of education is served, the school has an opportunity to hire another strong teacher, and the departing teacher will carry away positive feelings about the school and its administration. As in the old days when to be an incubator of heads was a bragging point for a school, to be a producer of fine teachers and administrators continues to be a sign of a school's vitality. Much as we missed teachers who left our school, I was always delighted and proud when they move onward and upward in the field of education.

Increasingly, those with an interest in taking on greater leadership roles in schools are able to find training opportunities to support their interests. Some, like the NAIS Fellowship for Aspiring Heads, are frankly directed at those with a specific goal, while a number of workshops around the country are aimed at sharpening the skills of the middle manager and administrators at the sub-head level. Professional development programs for administrative specialists—technology, admissions, college counseling, business office—are also plentiful, and offer both beginners and veterans exposure to new ideas and trends as well as the opportunity to make valuable personal and professional connections. Some high-end programs in the non-profit and business worlds provide training in specific leadership skills that can serve independent school educators well, and of course the many outstanding programs offered by the Klingenstein Center at Teachers College are specifically designed to turn fine educators into highly skilled leaders. Schools working to build the leadership capacity of their faculties actively promote such programs as excellent professional development opportunities. Schools reap a residual benefit when faculty members' names appear on the participant lists of programs that, like the Klingenstein Fellowships, are highly selective.

Many teachers elect, for reasons of their own, choose not to move into administration, and some even try it for a while (even as heads of school) and in the end step back into the classroom. Celebrate these teachers and their dedication to their calling.

We all know, and have been inspired by, teachers who seem more alive in the classroom than almost anywhere else. Anyone who has taught knows that a great class, with the students and the subject matter in a kind of magical synchrony, can be an adrenaline rush. For many teachers, the rush and the magic are revitalizing forces, and many people have noted the relative youthfulness of teachers when gathered among their coevals from other walks of life. The cares and concerns of the classroom teacher, focusing on their students and their curriculum, are about solving an endless series of human puzzles and watching the daily triumph of interest over indolence and engagement over ignorance.

I have known a few teachers who were once senior school administrators and either stepped or were forced away from "executive" positions. There has always been something a bit sad in their circumstances, a whispering of "You know, they used to be a ... ." How unfair! These individuals started out as excellent classroom teachers. They were raised to positions of relative grandeur precisely because of their energy and talent in the classroom, and in the end, sometimes in difficult circumstances, chose to return to the place where they were—and are—happiest. Spend a few minutes in their classrooms, or talk to their students—these are sometimes, and always in a quiet way, the most inspirational teachers of all. They bring a kind of wisdom to their work, and to their school communities, that is unlike almost any other. These reborn teachers can have a profound effect on the professional culture of the school, quietly mentoring and guiding younger teachers and providing a center of gravity to the faculty as a whole.

Teachers who choose to lead students toward self-awareness and the beauty of knowing and caring give an enormous gift to their students, their schools, and the world. The career choice of those who would rather do this work above all things, sacrificing pay and prestige, must be lauded, and the schools in which they work humbled by their efforts and their commitment. It is the duty of schools, through their culture, their professional development programs, and their mechanisms for providing material reward, to feed the flame that spurs these inspirational teachers.

Best Practices in Developing and Supporting Leadership

- Understand and respond to individual and collective faculty needs for growth and personal and professional satisfaction.

- Create opportunities for faculty members at all ages and stages of development to develop leadership skills and to implement their own ideas.

- Encourage the spirit of volunteerism through committees, grade-level teams, task forces, study groups, and other configurations of teachers collaborating in the development of school programs, policies, and practices.

- Recognize and reward teacher-leaders.

- Recognize, reward, and continue the training of "middle managers"—those involved in some supervisory or deliberative role.

- Weigh the costs and benefits of hiring from inside versus recruiting from outside in the development of middle-management leadership.

- Consider rotating some middle management or teacher-leader positions if the size and stability of the leadership pool warrants it.

- Weigh the costs and benefits of hiring for senior administrative positions; consider such issues as the potential for hurt feelings and the potential difficulty of supervising and evaluating former peers.

- Look for opportunities to increase individual leadership capacity through enrollment in workshops, courses, and leadership programs.

- Do not hold a faculty member or administrator back from looking for other positions if the opportunities for increased authority and responsibility in the school are limited.

- Respect and continue to support the work and development of faculty members who choose not to take on leadership roles; allow them to cultivate their professionalism as classroom teachers.

- Do not overlook the potential of former administrators who have chosen to return to the classroom; they represent a pool of wisdom, experience, and influence that can be of great value to a school.

Chapter Ten
Compensation

Maxim 10: Needs matter.

Several years ago I was asked to survey some of the ways in which independent schools were developing compensation programs designed to meet the needs of teachers at particular stages of their careers. The results of my research led to a self-evident and disheartening truth: schools with lots of resources—large endowments, wealthy and generous donor bases—can do the most to provide for the teachers in material ways. My interest in how the rest of North America's several thousand independent schools manage to hold on to their teachers in the absence of generous but not lavish pay and benefit schemes led directly to this book.

Even in our capitalist society, pride and a sense of professional satisfaction matter. To the highly skilled and highly educated sliver of the workforce that has chosen to become independent school educators, there are non-monetary factors, detailed previously, that draw teachers to schools and keep them there.

But compensation matters, too. It would be foolish to pretend otherwise. Statistics show the average compensation of teachers to be rising steadily in all regions, even approaching the pay levels of public school teachers in some areas. Salaries for starting teachers, especially, are no longer laughably low—although few young independent school teachers in affluent urban and suburban areas can afford to live without a roommate or two.

The situation for teachers is getting better. Recent reports suggest that the situation for administrators is getting better still, a strong incentive for some teachers to look for ways to leave the classroom to gain a better material quality of life.

A school should make every effort to keep its average compensation levels in line with regional averages and its benefit programs comparable to those of other schools. Schools that can pay more will have an easier time recruiting and retaining teachers than those that cannot or will not, and the ease will be relatively proportional. Not many schools continue to depress salaries at the entry level because "working here is a privilege," and gone are the days when numbers of independently wealthy teachers could be found instructing the children of affluence. Like that of students, the socioeconomic profile of independent school teachers has become more varied, and the size of the paycheck matters.

The customary veil of secrecy covering individual salaries survives perhaps more than it ought to, but many schools are working to demystify pay and develop transparent or at least intelligible and equitable compensation systems. Broad categories of scale concepts in use today include: step systems, where each year of experience and perhaps educational attainment involves an increase in pay; band systems, where teachers in particular bands of experience can expect payment within a stated range; point systems, in which experience, education, and job responsibilities are detailed and assigned monetary value; pay-for-performance systems that reward the entire faculty for the achievement of specified goals; and systems that offer the possibility of bonuses.

The "fear factor" for teachers around salary scales, at least where they have not been in place, is that in the transition to a scaled system any existing inequities will be erased (which is of course the whole point of the scale). Teachers who suspect that such inequities might be in their favor are understandably resistant to the thought of losing pay in the transition. The logical solution is to implement the scale over several years with the goal of bringing everyone *up* to the level of the preexisting "inequity." Highly paid teachers would simply receive smaller increases than those in the same cohort who were earning less.

For administrators, the potential "loss" in the implementation of a salary scale, beyond the whole question of smoothing out accumulated wrinkles in relative pay, is the ability to reward outstanding performance. The whole question of merit pay divides both the teaching profession—supervisors like it, the generality of teachers do not—and the general public, most of whom are convinced that good teachers should receive more money. The problem, of course, is establishing the criteria for "merit:" What demonstrable behaviors warrant increased monetary reward? And in whose hands does the decision lie to dole out this reward? And how much? Most heads of school or others who determine faculty pay annually jealously guard the right to tweak the pay of a "meritorious" teacher upward over peers, and most faculties acknowledge this right, probably in large part based on the hope that they will receive their fair share of the bounty over time. The code of "don't ask, don't tell" about pay prevails in many independent schools and enables the persistence of merit systems that are sometimes mysterious and occasionally sources of quiet rancor among faculty. It would be disingenuous not to acknowledge this.

The science of salary scales is evolving, but the key to any effective system of payment is to provide a living wage, to avoid both the appearance and reality of inequity, and to do whatever is possible to keep the school's overall level of compensation in at least plausible relation to peer schools. Any steps a school can take to develop published scales that still allow the school to acknowledge exemplary teacher performance will satisfy the interests of all.

Almost as important to the matter of compensation as the question of money is the nature of the agreement between the teacher and the school. Whether the agreement is a contract or a letter of agreement, the point is to protect the interests of both the teacher and the school and to specify the obligations of each toward the other. The key word here is "specify." Some teachers and many schools prefer a very general statements of these obligations, avoiding detailed job descriptions and noting only the position title, salary, and dates of service, perhaps with some other boilerplate and a reference to the employee handbook. Such agreements offer flexibility on both sides, although occasionally a line of boilerplate to the effect that the employee will complete "other duties as designated by the head of school" provides an umbrella under which the unexpected can occur.

Other schools are enamored of detailed job descriptions and complex contracts, looking to provide specificity of expectations and protection for the school against poor performance by the employee. The extent to which the nature of the contract becomes or does not become an element of litigation between schools and separated employees is hard to know. NAIS and the National Business Officers Association both offer resources relating to employment law and contract practices, but a school's own counsel is the best source of advice and guidance. There are also law firms, regionally and nationally, that offer expertise on independent school issues; a regional association could offer references.

Another way for schools to expand compensation for particularly expert or competent faculty and fund this compensation "outside" the normal salary line item is to develop a system of endowed chairs. Both the nature of endowments and the nature of the compensation itself can be structured in different ways, but a chair can carry its own endowment-generated salary or at least a stipend over and above the honor of being the chair holder. In this way the professional accomplishments of a teacher can be acknowledged and rewarded within a system that also provides significant giving opportunities for donors interested in supporting the academic program.

A general benefit that doubles as professional development involves large-scale grants for travel or study. Many such programs are supported by restricted or even external funds, and in some cases there are tight restrictions on the nature of the experience or work that can be sponsored. If the grants are well publicized and the applicants represent a variety of interests, ages, divisions, and career points, they can be of extraordinary value to the entire faculty over the long run. To receive a grant can be a point of personal pride, and the institution itself will benefit from the expanded or renewed excitement and knowledge of the recipient.

More and more, schools are discovering and devising ways to meet teachers' economic needs in other, less direct ways at various stages of their careers even as they work to raise general levels of compensation and to expand benefit policies.

Even before a teacher's service begins, the question of reimbursement for relocation expenses can arise. Relatively few schools provide generously in this area for journeyman teachers, even when they are moving from a distance, but for department heads or administrators schools may provide help, with the amount to be determined either on a case-by-case basis or by policy. This figure, usually subject to an upper limit, seems to be largely a matter of negotiation, although the establishment of a published policy would be beneficial.

For those just entering the profession, schools need to provide a living wage that will allow teachers, whether in a dormitory or working in a day school, to live independently. This can be accomplished most readily through a reasonable starting salary, although other ways to sweeten the pot for beginning teachers can include a system for helping the teacher pay down student loans or some kind of support for graduate education. All of these come with a relatively high price tag, although tying the program to longevity-based incentives can allow a school to amortize the cost over a period of years.

Housing benefits come in various forms. Boarding schools require many faculty to live in dormitories, a benefit in an expensive housing market but a burden in rural areas where real estate prices are low. A number of day schools offer housing to faculty on bases ranging from market-value rent to no-cost, although housing offered at below market rate is a taxable benefit when it is unrelated to the needs of the job. Schools have made some forays into offering housing bonuses or low-cost mortgage loans to teachers, although some consider using endowment funds in this way, even for the benefit of the school's faculty, to be a questionable stewardship practice when the loan rate falls significantly below the rate of return that the endowment could be earning.

Typically the allocation of available housing made using some combination of seniority, household size (the family needs to fit into the space available), and the needs of the school. Whether housing is regarded as a benefit or a burden, whatever method the school uses to decide who lives where needs to be clear and free of any appearance of favoritism or conflict of interest. Perfect solutions can seldom be found, but minimizing sources of rancor related to the allocation of major benefits serves the interests of both school and faculty.

Other ways that schools can help support faculty include opportunities for seasonal or ancillary employment as summer program staff or even on a building and grounds or painting crew. Some schools that support extensive student travel programs invite teacher-chaperones to act as entrepreneurs, although the arrangement of liability responsibility for such trips can be complex. Stipends for coaches or activity leaders also can be used to provide additional compensation, a sort of "fee for service" arrangement that is anathema to some schools and *de rigueur* in others.

Along with travel programs, schools can arrange remunerative situations for teachers in other ways. Some make arrangements with families or alumni to offer seasonal employment to faculty members, from baby- or house-sitting to office, construction, or industrial work. Many schools do not object to teachers tutoring students from the school for a fee, except those in their own classes or possibly divisions or disciplines. Sensibly arranged, tutoring can become an easy way for teachers to acquire some added income, although all potential for conflicts of interest (some would aver that teachers tutoring students from their own school is in and of itself such a conflict) should be avoided.

It should be noted that there are those who will disagree violently with these suggestions, and for reasons that should be acknowledged. A school should encourage or even allow private financial arrangements between faculty members and student families only with a full understanding of the vulnerabilities that a position of economic dependency can exploit. The teacher in a subservient position or, potentially more dangerous, who feels indebted to a family might well find it difficult to maintain professional boundaries in situations when hard decisions must be made.

A number of schools have also enlisted the support of families, alums, and friends of the school to provide other material benefits to faculty. These may involve discounted or "professional courtesy" rate services or the donation of tickets to events or even the use of vacation homes. An objection could be made to such arrangements if they are not generally known or available to all faculty and staff, in which they become nothing more than acts of personal generosity toward a particular teacher or group of teachers. A number of schools have articulated specific faculty gift policies to forestall situations in which a beneficiary teacher might feel obliged to return a favor in the form of preferential treatment for a child.

Limitations on the size and form of gifts to individual faculty members from individual families seem in order for other reasons, as well; anything representing a competition or families trying to out-do one another, with holiday gifts for example, can put both teachers and less affluent families in extremely uncomfortable positions. The hundred-dollar gift certificate to a spa from Sammy Smith's family might not only seem excessive to Ms. Johnson, the teacher (although indeed she might be looking forward to using it), it may also make Sammy's classmate Judy Jones feel ashamed of her gift of a paper plate of home-baked cookies. Better the Smiths be told that the gift certificate would make a wonderful donation to the silent auction to support professional development and that a sincere note of gratitude—and perhaps some home-baked cookies—will be a sufficient present for the teacher.

Historically there have been schools that have developed systems to reward outstanding teachers on an annual basis with what are essentially hefty (four-figure) cash bonuses, either described as such or presented as grants. While these may have a fine moral effect on faculty, especially those receiving them, it is important that a school contemplating such a program develops a fair system to determine who will receive them; faculty committees of rotating membership seem to work well. Because they are tied explicitly to performance, the bonuses must be given to those whose performance is obviously exceptional. Over time, the bounty must be widely, generously, and deservingly spread out to avoid any appearance of favoritism.

Younger teachers will probably not be the ones clamoring for health care, dental care, long-term disability insurance, or hefty pension fund contributions, but the options should be there as soon as possible for faculty to participate in all of these. Although schools continue to delay eligibility for pension programs, in particular, for one or more years after the start of employment, younger employees should be educated in the long-term value of retirement funds invested early.

There is a sometimes-contentious debate about the degree to which schools determine or limit the amount of choice in benefit programs. While economics constrain the number of options schools can offer, many teachers would like to be able to make more decisions with regard to bout retirement plans and the nature of the investments made by their vendors. Along with more traditional plans with limited choice, more flexible menus of benefit options are being offered by a number of schools. The challenge remains to provide sufficient long-term security for faculty without removing them from the decision-making process completely. Some regional associations have been active in assembling groups for health and dental plans as well. Other benefits offered by smaller numbers of schools include reduced-rate insurance of various kinds. The basic expectation, however, is still paid individual health insurance for the teacher and a pension plan to which the school contributes a set amount, sometimes rising with years of service.

As teachers' households grow, another key benefit is health or dental coverage for spouses or partners. State requirements vary, but same-sex domestic partner benefits are as common as spousal benefits in many areas. Some contribution by the school toward partner or family health insurance premiums is no longer an unreasonable expectation, although the dizzying rise in the cost of health insurance may jeopardize this practice.

Related to this comes the matter of benefits for or related to children. The Federal Family and Medical Leave Act specifies the amount of unpaid time employees may receive for maternity, paternity, adoption, care of an immediate family member, or to deal with their own medical needs, but many schools offer more, either with pay or without, up to a term or a whole year of unpaid leave. Along with health insurance, dental insurance is in high demand but not commonly provided. Employer-sponsored programs that allow teachers to set aside pre-tax earnings for child-care expenses (older teachers may want the same for dependent at-home parents) are the simplest ways for schools to assist faculty with this expense, although some schools provide on-campus fee-for-service childcare. This is an enormous resource and regulatory expense but worth it if the number of faculty children is large or if enrollment—perhaps at a higher fee structure—can be extended to the general public. Reduced-fee enrollment in the school's ancillary programs—or in the programs of a consortium of schools, if such a congenial group can be assembled to share benefits and resources—is another benefit that can be offered at little cost.

The Mother of All Benefits, of course, is tuition remission. No issue can be more fraught with emotion and potential for divisiveness, especially when any change in an existing policy is contemplated. Many teachers without children see the benefit as unfair and discriminatory. Those with children see it as loaded with personal and even political importance, and the argument that a teacher's children ought to have access to the school where the parent works is compelling. Remission policies, if the school's faculty is culturally or racially diverse, can contribute to a school's diversity efforts and at the very least such a policy supports a degree of socioeconomic diversity. In addition, tuition remission can be a powerful factor in creating a sense of being valued and included among all faculty, participants or not.

Remission schemes range from "full rides" for faculty children—some single-gender schools go so far as to offer the same level of support to opposite-gender faculty children at other schools—to no remission at all. Commonly used policies are based on: years of service; a flat percentage of salary; a percentage of the total financial aid budget or tuition revenue line divided by the number of faculty children (which can lead to wild year-to-year variations for a particular family); and a flat fee, which may or may not decrease if there is more than one child from the same family. One method calculates a financial aid award based on the family income not including any income from the school. This system does appropriately aid single parents and two-teacher households, but the statistical likelihood that a male non-teacher wage earner will earn more than a female (thus yielding a smaller award) shades this system slightly against female teachers. Standard and recommended procedure involves accounting tuition remission, like all financial aid, as an expense.

All the arguments for and against remission boil down to the financial needs of the school versus the school's willingness to provide a costly benefit to faculty. A school with relatively meager resources or vast numbers of faculty children, either at the school or coming along, can perhaps be excused for taking a conservative stance relative to this benefit. Regional norms play a role in what might be expected at a given school, as well. Schools that decide to make a reduction in an existing program can generate firestorms of faculty *angst* and anger, as happens whenever an expectation is dashed. Even so, and I write with the bias of a parent in favor of generous remission programs, the actual value of tuition remission as a benefit that inspires retention may be questionable. Anecdotal evidence suggests that a generous retention program may attract teachers, but that relatively few choose to change jobs because of the absence of a policy or because support is reduced. The latter circumstance can, it is worth repeating, cause trouble; the creation of tiered or grandfathered schemes is an alternative to sudden, sweeping change.

Another benefit area whose existence can clearly express a school's willingness to care for its faculty is the Employee Assistance Program. While some schools would, not surprisingly, jettison faculty whose mental illness or abuse of alcohol or other substances impinges on their performance—and indeed, showing up to class "under the influence" would constitute cause for immediate dismissal in most situations—increasingly both case law and developing notions of the nature of mental illness and alcoholism or other kinds of dependencies suggest that these conditions approach or even fall into the category of disability. Some schools spell out the nature of the support they will provide to a staff member struggling with an issue of this sort, going so far as to underwrite treatment programs and to offer medical leaves of absence for this purpose. At the less elaborate end of the spectrum, some schools have offered anti-smoking programs for staff (and even students).

Whether or not they should be classified as part of a school's salary and benefit program or whether they are an aspect of school culture, what might be called "collective benefits" are in a category by themselves. These would include union representation for faculty and the associated practice of collective bargaining and such less comprehensive practices as faculty representation on the Board. A minority of schools have voting representatives from the faculty, and Boards and administrations have traditionally been cautious lest Jacobin tendencies be released, but in general schools with full faculty representation probably experience no more or less conflict than those without. The presence of a non-administrative faculty observer or even one or more voting members at Board meetings can create a valuable foundation of mutual understanding and respect, and faculty on Board committees can be sources of useful and even necessary perspectives and ideas. In the end, the establishment of healthy working relationships between a school's faculty and its governing bodies (making certain that each party is aware of lines of authority and responsibility) can only improve the climate of the school as a workplace and as a place of shared vision.

As they approach their own middle age, many teachers struggle with the aging and illness of their own parents and older family members. Pre-tax set-asides for dependent care expenses should be encouraged for faculty facing this challenge, and making clear to faculty the school's policies about family leave—whatever is over and above the statutory minimum—helps people in a complicated bind know where they stand with their employer. Obviously, compassionate leave and, more importantly, genuine expressions and acts of compassion can do much to ease anxieties. Schools with religious affiliations may be able to connect faculty with resources for the care and housing of family members with diminished ability to provide for themselves.

A sabbatical program for teachers may be considered a professional development tool as much as a benefit. Schools with these programs have found many ways both to structure leaves and to determine eligibility. Affluent schools may be able to offer a traditional "every seventh year" sabbatical, but most plans are based on some combination of seniority and the quality of an application. A few schools place no restriction on sabbatical recipients' programs, but most ask that the work done while on a leave—a term, a half-year, or a full year at some proportion of salary—be in some way related to professional growth.

As teachers edge toward retirement themselves, benefits like pension programs, disability insurance, and life insurance become more attractive. Schools would do well to educate teachers of all ages often and early in all aspects of retirement planning, and many schools offer financial planning assistance to faculty as part of their benefit package or their human resources office.

Many teachers consider changing schools as retirement looms, either to reduce their responsibilities with age, to cut back to part-time, or to relocate nearer the site of their planned retirement. In many cases this involves what is presented as "taking early retirement" at the school they are leaving. If this is literally true, the teacher needs to be assisted with completing the necessary paperwork to prepare for receiving pension or retirement payments—as well as educated on income restrictions and other regulations relating to post-retirement employment. Again, this process could be a part of general financial planning assistance.

For the school, teachers seeking to change jobs in anticipation of retirement can represent a desirable hiring opportunity. An interesting phenomenon occurring in certain popular retirement destinations involves older, empty-nest teaching couples taking jobs for a few years in the "triple threat" capacity—that they had perhaps not filled for 25 years—while establishing themselves in the geographical area in anticipation of actual retirement.

How far the school is willing to make a benefit program extend in support of teachers who have truly retired can be, like tuition remission, a complex issue. Whether a school is willing to allow retired faculty to participate in any of the school's benefit programs or perquisites, or whether a retired teacher living near the school is still able to take meals on campus or enjoy complimentary admission to school events is a matter for the school to decide and, in the end, a reflection on the school's overall attitude toward its faculty.

It may seem paternalistic for the school to take an active interest in helping a teacher nearing retirement age to make plans and organize aspects of the coming event, and many teachers will need no assistance whatever. As a colleague long ago once remarked regarding the failure of a Board to appoint a faculty member to its finance committee, "Independent school teachers manage to live upper-middle-class lives on a lower-middle-class incomes, and we're pretty darn good at financial planning." The heartbreaking stories of forty years ago involving boarding school faculty with literally no place to go upon retirement are unusual today, but everyone— teachers, administrators, heads—of a certain age should be giving serious thought to the resources that will be available to them as their careers wind down.

Best Practices
in Compensation

- Keep average salaries and benefits in line with those of peer schools and with other schools in the region; obviously, the higher the percentile a school can occupy, the greater its chances of recruiting and retaining the teachers it wants.

- Pay particular to the salaries of beginning teachers, and do whatever is possible to ensure them a living wage and as much independence as possible.

- Consider the establishment of a salary scale using any of the existing models or a system unique to the needs and capacities of the school.

- Develop and make use of multiple-year contracts, job descriptions, and/or contract language that meet the needs and fit the culture of the school; ultra-specific language can be limiting, too-broad language can invite abuse.

- Consider ways outside the normal salary line to increase financial rewards for teachers:

    - Use endowed chairs as mechanisms for underwriting the compensation of exceptional teachers

- Look for opportunities to provide employment to teachers through ancillary programs—tutoring, standardized test supervision, building and grounds work during vacations

- Enlist student families, alumni, and friends of the school as potential sources of small benefits for faculty—seasonal employment, tickets to events and cultural venues, discounted professional services; such benefits should be available to all staff members, and below-market-value benefits of very high value may be considered taxable gifts

- Consider the establishment of a gift policy to limit the value and nature of gifts from student families.

- Develop a flexible menu of benefits that responds to the ages and stages of faculty members, but vigorously promote participation in a pension or retirement program among all faculty.

- Consider expanding benefit programs to include:

  - dental insurance, where feasible

  - a policy on reimbursement for moving expenses

- various kinds of insurance at group or discounted rates
- financial planning assistance
- a comprehensive Employee Assistance Plan
- maternity/paternity/adoption and family and compassionate leave benefits in excess of the statutory minimum
- "sabbaticals" of a length, frequency, and nature that school sees as commensurate with its goals and its resources

- Consider a program for helping younger faculty pay down student loans or to reimburse faculty for graduate education; a stepped, after-the-fact program can be economical as well as helping to ensure retention.

- Consider a program involving either cash bonuses or no-strings travel or study grants, but award such grants in a way that ensures equity and confirms an impression of "proportional reward" in the faculty community (that is, make sure that such funds are allocated to those who deserve them).

- Allocate school housing in a way that avoids to the degree possible any possible impression of favoritism or cronyism.

- Tuition remission or financial aid for faculty children should be as generous and equitable as possible; make changes to existing programs in ways that neither promote inequity nor impose sudden, unanticipated shock on faculty family resources.

- Offer and vigorously promote programs allowing faculty to set aside pre-tax income to pay for medical or dependent-care expenses.

- Encourage all faculty to begin financial planning as soon as possible, even if financial planning assistance is not a part of the school's benefit package.

- Consider the potential benefits of faculty representation on the school's governing bodies or on Board committees relating to finance.

Chapter Eleven
Senior Faculty

Maxim 11: Old dogs need new tricks.

I have observed in schools a great disparity in the ways that different teachers approach the last decade or so of their careers. Some go out sailing, as it were, as enthralled by their students and their work as they were in their first days in the classroom. As teacher-leaders and as cultural cornerstones in their schools, they gain in confidence and capacity as they age, and their reputations and presence expand like those of Mr. Chips himself. There are times when it is not so bad to be living a cliché, and this is one example.

The art of keeping teachers like this engaged is not as simple as it may seem; the trick is not to take their competence and enthusiasm for granted. The school must learn to look for appropriate opportunities to take advantage of them as a teacher-leaders and to honor their wisdom about program and students. If the school has a mechanism for recognizing the work of great teachers in a formal way, such as an award, an endowed chair, or a travel or sabbatical program with an honorary flavor, a teacher will presumably receive it at some point. The teacher might be an ideal nominee for one of the "teacher of the year" awards sponsored by national organizations.

External professional development for valued senior faculty should be a priority. These teachers might be steered toward funded, high-prestige programs like the National Endowment for the Humanities summer seminars or Klingenstein Fellowships. If they have areas of strong interest, related programs should be identified and senior faculty teachers encouraged to attend (underwritten by the school as necessary). There are also a number of programs aimed at experienced teachers, some offered by regional associations.

The literature of leadership has produced several worthwhile volumes that might be of interest to schools looking for ways to further harness the energies of a highly competent but administration-shy teacher or two. *Leading Quietly*, by Harvard Business School professor Joseph Badaracco is less a how-to manual than a meditation on the ways that those in less-than-autocratic positions can effect positive leadership in both moral and practical contexts. Some of the work of Michael Fullan, a University of Toronto-based educational leadership guru, also addresses ways in which senior leadership can exert a powerful moral influence on a school community. The *Horace* series by Theodore Sizer, although not about leadership *per se*, shows how committed teachers can effect positive and even radical change in a school community. Any of these books might prove interesting and inspiring reading for senior faculty and in any event are worthy of a place in a school's professional development library.

The positive, energetic, and productive senior teacher is a living treasure to their school. For other teachers, though, the latter days of a career are a struggle. For whatever reason, the fires that once burned brightly and illuminated classroom manner, relationships with students, and real excitement about the whole idea of teaching have begun to flicker and dim. Optimism has been replaced by occasional outbursts of cynicism, and some of these teachers can be counted on to disappear whenever discussions of new ideas and new initiatives take place. A few become truly bitter, doing their jobs competently but grudgingly even as they build a small following among other unhappy—often young and inexperienced in the ways of work—faculty.

The picture can be bleak, and yet...

And yet. Over the years the teacher has given enormously to the school and to students. The school has put great trust and many resources into this person and been repaid many times over. There may be hordes of alums who come back to the school just to check in with this teacher, and their advisees may be paragons of lifetime loyalty. It is only in the relationship with the institution that things have begun to go sour.

The warning signs are probably clear, at least in retrospect. In some cases the teacher is harboring feelings of disappointment or frustration over an ambition that has somehow been thwarted—by the school or not—or a dream whose fulfillment now seems impossible. Perhaps a personal situation has been difficult—an aging parent, marital strife, a child's illness, perhaps even alcohol abuse. In any event, whatever mechanisms the school can muster to offer support, up to and including counseling or, in dire need, the application of an Employee Assistance Program or even the offer of a leave of absence. A school that can be discreetly proactive in addressing faculty members' personal crises (no matter what their ages) and providing thorough support when it is needed is demonstrating the quality of its "culture of concern" in a powerful way. Whether this support forestalls later disaffection or not, it is simply the right thing to do.

A teacher who has been turned down for some type of internal promotion is vulnerable to feelings of frustration or even anger. It may be that these feelings will inspire the teacher to leave, but a surprising number of disappointed candidates remain at their schools. Many manage the situation with equanimity and seek other ways in which they can make some sort of change in their working situation, while others may pass through a sullen period. Some sort of informal counseling—from a peer or from an administrative friend not associated with the disappointing decision—can help, and here the school can attempt to do for the teacher what some teachers can do for themselves: look for and gently suggest other places where the teacher can apply their talents in new and satisfying ways. If these alternatives have real substance, the offer is a much-needed vote of confidence for the teacher.

In other circumstances the teacher is responding to some sort of change, perceived or real, in the direction or values of the school. The "problem" may be a new policy or curriculum initiative, or it may be the style of a new administrator. The teacher may feel as though they are being asked to make a major change in classroom practice or to compromise a deeply held principle. Mandated integration of technology has a reputation as the Waterloo of some veteran independent school teachers, making a strong argument for differentiated by faculty-wide training in this and other emerging areas of novel practice. Teachers for whom any new way of doing things has been a challenge will not be able to develop much further until they have been shown the practical value of the new skill or practice, and they need to be quietly singled out for the best and most supportive training the school can provide. All the eye-rolling in the world by frustrated technology specialists or academic administrators will not alter a teacher's practice, but focused instruction emphasizing the value of what is being learned may.

Far-reaching and personally challenging work in the area of diversity or anti-bias training can cause angry defensive walls to rise if teachers feel as though discussions of institutional racism or white privilege, for example, are calling their own intentions and attitudes into question. The teacher who maintains that they don't care "if my students are black or white or green or purple" may simply be a child of an earlier time, when progressive, well-intentioned attitudes toward race favored a "color-blind" stance. Our understanding of the meaning of multiculturalism in schools has become more sophisticated, and we now acknowledge and address issues of difference as a central aspect of our practice. But for the teacher who came into teaching when another set of equally well thought-out values was in effect, feelings of dislocation and defensiveness surface when what was once seen as right-mindedness is labeled as wrong, or worse. The teacher needs to be brought along, and can be, but failing to acknowledge their good will only exacerbate the problem.

The case of teachers resistant to institutional change is particularly difficult, and sometimes the school simply needs to move forward and give the reluctant teacher an ultimatum. But the management of change itself, according to Robert Evans in *The Human Side of School Change*, is a complex task that should not be given short shrift when a school sets about altering important practices or changing direction. Even a change at the senior administrative level can unbalance apparently steady and productive members of the faculty. What Evans and others do assert, however, is that meaningful institutional change cannot be made while "working around" a resistant teacher; at some point the question must be called.

Sometimes the teacher's drift just happens, and at some point others in the school become aware that a colleague is struggling. Even if there is evidence of some sort of animosity, someone—probably the head of school—needs to address the issue before it grows worse. The decision to confront the teacher (or not) and how to make the approach is a delicate one, but at stake is the career of a valued faculty member as well as the well-being of the school. This is not an easy matter. The approach must be made in as positive and concerned a tone as possible, and should be based on some sort of clear evidence or, at the very least, a series of "I-statements," as in "I have noticed that...." It is quite likely that the teacher will at first deny the issue, but the administration must persist—gently, with accurate, non-accusatory language, and in a helpful tone.

In truth, there is no guarantee that anything the school or anyone in it can do to bring a disaffected teacher back into the fold. Experience, however, tells us that ignoring the situation, becoming quietly angry at the person without sharing misgivings, or simply trying to tiptoe around the teacher and their perceived "issues" will accomplish nothing. The continued application of positive energy to the situation, if sincerely done, has the potential to make matters better. Whether in the end the teacher will accept support or even talk about whatever may be causing the drift or distress, the school must make the good-faith effort. As they are for the teacher who is soaring, recognition, meaningful new work, and even the prospect of legitimately earned reward are major components of the *materia medica* of the healing process for the teacher with a wounded soul or psyche or who is just plain angry.

If it becomes apparent that there is no way to ameliorate the situation, the school faces a difficult choice. The preferred solution to such a dilemma is to counsel the teacher out, suggesting that the match between teacher and school is no longer conducive to enthusiastic work or personal satisfaction. Whatever resources the school can bring to bear on making a separation under these circumstances a positive one should be used: assistance in finding a new position, financial planning assistance toward taking early retirement, if feasible, and perhaps even some form of severance.

The other course of action is much more difficult. In the absence of demonstrated or observed professional incompetence or malfeasance, there may be no way to develop a case to "fire" the teacher, although an evaluation category relating to support of the school's mission and values can serve as a blanket to cover actions seen necessary for the good of the school and its students. Instead, the matter becomes one of setting specific, written goals with clearly stated consequences for non-compliance, in serious cases presented as a contract requiring the employee's signed agreement. Distasteful and painful as such a process can be, it may be the only way to get the teacher's attention and to draw them back into the realm of satisfactory performance.

The most effective way for a school to avoid having teachers flicker and fade, of course, is to attend to their needs and their interests at all ages and stages of their personal and professional development. Old dogs can, in fact, learn new tricks, and they need to. The school that forgets this or at some point focuses attention on the needs or the perceived greater promise of less experienced faculty at the expense of veterans can run into trouble. The school's professional culture and professional development program must not have gaps in their relevance to teachers at any level. Schools at all times must consciously be looking for ideas and opportunities that will engage and inspire all members of their faculties.

Best Practices
in Managing Senior Faculty

- Recognize and reward the meritorious or exemplary service and enthusiasm of senior faculty to the extent possible using endowed chairs; school awards or grants; "special" sabbaticals or travel grants; external recognition, such as nomination for "Teacher of the Year" awards or selective fellowships or study programs.

- Look for special workshops for experienced teachers in the independent school world as ways to recognize and invigorate exemplary and enthusiastic senior faculty.

- Look to the literature of leadership in both the business and education sectors for ways to inspire exemplary and enthusiastic senior faculty.

- Learn to look for and recognize signs of developing unhappiness, cynicism, or diminished performance among senior faculty; respond as the situation requires. To do this:
  - Be sensitive to the sources of the teacher's difficulties; whether they are personal or school-related matters

- Find ways to support the teacher if there are personal issues that can be alleviated by institutional assistance or the help of individual community members
- If the situation threatens the well-being of the community, confront the teacher as soon as possible; be supportive, not dismissive
- If the situation involves change within the school, look for ways to help the teacher cope; if the teacher's unhappiness and resistance are entrenched, then be prepared to counsel the teacher out; enabling and working around non-compliance is inconsistent with the achievement of major change in a school
- If the teacher insists on remaining, set clear goals for improved performance and state unequivocal consequences for failure, within the framework of the school's stated employment policies and practices
- Identify ways in which a "fading" teacher might be reinvigorated through recognition, reward, or professional development.
- Consider the implementation of early retirement or severance packages for senior

faculty whose efficacy is diminished and who cannot seem to be re-energized.

- Avoid difficult situations in the first place by developing a professional culture that recognizes and energizes each teacher at each stage of their development.

Chapter Twelve
Endings

Maxim 12: All things must end.

The literature on the separation of teachers at any stage of their careers is, not surprisingly, rather thin. Because the departure of any teacher from any school is a personal, unique event, it can take many forms and occur for many reasons. It does not always occur voluntarily (on the teacher's part, that is), and so matters of confidentiality and even legal repercussions rear their heads. However the ending comes to pass, the object is to create as little negative and as much positive impact as possible.

"Counseling out" a senior teacher of diminishing efficacy or the dismissal of teachers for cause are probably the two most traumatic circumstances in someone can be asked to leave a school, but there are ways to minimize negative impact. In the case of the senior teacher being counseled out, either to retirement, to an indeterminate "sabbatical," or to another job in the field of education, it is appropriate to express sincere appreciation for the teacher's contributions to the school. Even if the circumstances of the departure are clear (and inevitably they will be to many people in the community), the contributions are real, as is the affection that many people will feel toward the teacher. If the teacher balks at the making of an official fuss, the school should do whatever it can to enlist their friends and supporters in the planning of a tasteful, positive "unofficial" but clearly school-supported event to honor the teacher at this point of transition. There may be awkward moments, and those with less than positive relationships with the teacher should have the tact to steer clear— although the head of school must in any circumstance play at least a brief ceremonial role in whatever is done.

For the teacher suddenly dismissed for cause, specific circumstances will dictate the school's actions. In general, communication with the school community should be made as soon as possible, and the nature of the situation should be spelled out as specifically and fully as legal counsel will permit. Although this may fly in the face of a school's desire to smooth over the incident and move on, an official statement developed by the head, the crisis team (if need be), and the school's attorney will go far toward staving off a torrent of rumors, most of them suggesting things far worse than whatever actually happened. The most careful attention must be paid to students, who, no matter what their age, will have difficulty understanding aspects of the situation and who will need reassurance based on as much truth as can be made public. In some cases the reassurance will have to be that their teacher was treated appropriately, while in others it will relate to the students' own sense of safety and security. Often it is both.

When a teacher's malfeasance invokes the legal process, either civil or criminal, the school's "performance" must be letter-perfect both with regard to meeting its own legal responsibilities and to the protection of its own interests and those of its students. It would not be far-fetched for the school to engage public relations counsel skilled in managing adverse situations to help. The point is not to cover up but to enable the school to continue to serve students with as little distraction as possible.

Less challenging but by no means less important is the case of a younger or mid-career teacher who is not asked back for reasons relating to evaluated performance. When and how and to whom the announcement of the departure will be made may be a significant issue, and here again students and families may need reassurance as to the reasons for the departure. If the teacher has been especially popular, the nature of the announcement and the reasons presented may require careful engineering.

A teacher leaving to return to school, to change careers, or to take another teaching position should be specifically honored to the extent appropriate. Schools can face a challenging situation when the leaving "class" of teachers includes both wildly popular and not-so-well-regarded members, and at least on an institutional level there must be a serious attempt made to assure parity in the scale of the official recognition. Many schools have a traditional event to say farewell to departing faculty, and, no matter what the circumstances of each departure, the amount of verbiage, attention, and the material quality of any good-bye gifts given must be apportioned more on the basis of years of service than on popularity (whether it be with colleagues, students, or the administration). Those who wish to do more will find other circumstances in which to do so, but the school in its official attitudes must be positive and generous to an equal degree about all departing faculty.

An ending that calls for a serious response is the loss of a faculty member to death or long-term disability or disease. Regardless of the cause of the loss, the entire school community must be acknowledged to be in a state of grieving, and there is seldom time to prepare for this. A school's crisis planning must include identifying the resources and procedures that will be put in place in such a situation, and lining up specialists—counselors, grief therapists—should be done long before need arises. Regional independent school associations or peer schools can offer advice in this area. Here again, it is students whose interest must be consulted first, but colleagues, too, will have varying and unpredictable responses to the loss or disability of a peer. Close watch should be kept on the faculty in order to be able to initiate specific interventions if they are needed. Painful as such a loss is, it offers an opportunity for the school to come together around its values and its rituals. A school with a positive professional culture and a straightforward, respectful community will be able to help itself through almost any crisis.

Ideally, a teacher leaving the school should be doing so through a long-planned and voluntary retirement. Some schools have offered "early retirement" or "buy-out" options based on age or years of service, but these are generally put in place to meet institutional needs: to create opportunities for new faculty hiring, simply to lure a particular individual out of the school, and even to downsize. Teachers taking these options should be honored just as all other retiring teachers would be honored, but the occasion of a more traditional and voluntary retirement, particularly of a teacher with long years of service to the school or at least in education, is a milestone that requires special attention.

Many of the teachers whom I have watched retire over the years have displayed an extraordinary modesty. I think that many of them would have preferred to slip out the door in June unnoticed and unremarked. I have great respect for this attitude and tried hard to pull off my own retirement in just such a fashion, but the fact is, the retirement of a teacher matters on many levels.

First of all, a teacher who has given much over a period of many years is a model for all other teachers. Such service has involved considerable sacrifice, especially for those now retiring who began teaching during the 1970s and even the 1960s, when independent schools asked much and paid little. The teacher may have been, consciously or not, a mentor to many others, and there may be dozens of aspects of the school's policies and practices that bear the stamp of their influence. In retirement, the teacher brings attention to these worthy acts.

Second, the retiring teacher leaves behind a legacy of students influenced. Whether the teacher was truly charismatic or a bit of a *prima donna*, generations of students have been entranced by their talents and manner. Even if the teacher has been more reserved nature, there are students who returned the teacher's interest in them with their own quiet respect and attention. As the teacher prepares to leave the classroom, we are reminded of the good they have done with students in ways seen and unseen, acknowledged and unacknowledged.

Finally, the teacher who is retiring will take a piece of the fabric of the school along. A teacher cannot work long and hard in any institution without in the end both becoming that institution and having the institution become them. The teacher may have wrestled to the end with administrators about this or that issue, or have been famously averse to attending sporting events, or been the last teacher to sneak off campus during a free period to sneak a cigarette, but these are the acts of a personality who has made peace with a school and who is willing to live out this peace with integrity. The school that has wrestled back and that has known when to humor and when to honor this personality is proclaiming the depth and breadth of its own spirit and its own humanity.

It matters little exactly what the school does for the teacher who is retiring in a blaze of glory; some can do much, others less. A cash gift raised by alumni, a lifetime ticket to the school's arts center, a school chair, or a set of golf clubs—the intent is what matters and what must be communicated. The events around the retirement must be a proclamation of the school's values and its respect for the members of its community and above all for its teachers.

The school, through whatever benefit plans it might administer into a teacher's period of retirement, continues to hold some responsibility for the teacher, and it is a paltry place indeed that does not find ways to include former faculty in events and on mailing lists (including, of course, that of the development office). Some schools maintain a roster of faculty emeriti, sustaining the honor of association in perpetuity, and other forms of honor—named gifts relating to special interests of the teacher, distinguished service awards—can be created as well. In a few cases schools have created special positions for retired faculty, such as archivist or school historian, that allow a teacher a continuing connection with the campus and the school community.

For the school, a retirement is above all a mirror. The thoughtful school will regard itself in this mirror carefully, if just for a moment, taking stock of good points and bad, of blemishes and beauty marks. The thoughtful school will glean from this self-examination a bit of information about what it can do better next time to serve its faculty and its students.

In the end, there is a beginning. The retiring teacher departs, and the school embarks on a quest to find someone new for the same position. The school has suffered a loss that it must bear as it can. It also has been given an opportunity to take all that it has learned to heart, and, in recruiting, hiring, and retaining the next round of teachers, to become stronger still.

An afterthought: There may be no happier way to end this book than by referring the reader to Parker Palmer's *The Courage to Teach*, a celebration of teaching and teachers that moved even the hard heart of this old teacher. It reminds the reader just what the value of a good teacher can be, and it can be mined for meaningful—and truthful—quotes that will make any retirement ceremony the ode to joy that it should be.

Best Practices
in Managing Endings

- Unless a departure is sudden and difficult, recognize all departing teachers officially in proportion to their years of service, not their popularity; even teachers being counseled out deserve the thanks and recognition being given their coevals.

- In the case of sudden dismissals, communicate clearly as much as is prudent as widely as necessary and as swiftly as possible; explain enough to forestall rumor and to protect the rights of all parties. The school's first duty is to reassure students and other community members and protect them from damaging rumor. Seek guidance from counsel.

- Prepare for the eventuality of the loss of a faculty member by death, injury, or serious illness by lining up appropriate resources (grief specialists, counselors) as part of the school's crisis plan; when the worst happens, carefully observe students and faculty and provide the support they need.

- Use a school's values, rituals, and traditions to reinforce the bonds of community in the aftermath of a crisis or loss.

- When a long-term, senior teacher retires, recognize the impact of the impending loss on the teacher, on the school as an institution, on the rest of the faculty, on students, and on the profession.

- Do for the retiring teacher all that is possible materially and symbolically, and honor their service in the highest possible terms.

- Consider the creation of a category of "faculty emeritus" or other ways to symbolically or in fact sustain the connection between a valued retiring teacher and the school.

ACKNOWLEDGMENTS

My great gratitude goes to all who have in any way contributed to my understanding of the teaching profession and to the writing of this book:

- Those who have been so kind as to communicate with me about some aspect teaching and learning and who have generously shared with me anecdotes, advice, and/or resources from their own schools, organizations, and experiences: Dory Adams, Leslie Altman, Mimi Baer, Rick Bauer, Marc Bisson, Tina Blythe, Ben Bolte, Rachel Brown, Robert Bryan, Tom Carroll, Steve Clem, Stephen Clement, Toast Coley, Orpheus Crutchfield, Jennifer Darrah, Dave Davies, Len Doran, Mike Downs, Jim Dunaway, Don Firke, Nancy Fox, Julie Gabriele, Eric Gold, John Gulla, Anne Henry, Janice Hubbard, Tim Fish, Lynn Friedman, Robert Hallett, Sarah Hanawald, Laurie Hinrichs, James Holmes, Bill Ivey, Sarah Jencks, Simon Jeynes, Frank Jones, Kathleen Jordan, Damon Kerby, Philip Keywood, Cleve Latham, Cheryl Little, Elise London, Joan Lonergan, Steven McCollum, Marie McEntee, John Meehl, Lisa Merryman, Peter Nilsson, Kate

Olena, Mary Pleasanton, Jim Pugh, Sean Raymond, Stuart Remensnyder, Laura Robertson, Elizabeth Sky-McIlvain, Bill Stephenson, Peter Tacy, Chris Thinnes, Mike Vachow, Dietrich von Schwerdtner, and Jon White

- The authors of various writings and presentations that have been instrumental or inspirational in this project: Dick Barbieri, Roland Barth, Patrick Bassett, Jerome Bruner, Wendy Davenson, Gerald Devlin, Robert Evans, Sharon Feiman-Nemser, Ned Hallowell, Brendan Halpin, Richard Ingersoll, Rob Kennedy, Susan Moore Johnson and her colleagues at the Project for the Next Generation of Teachers at the Harvard Graduate School of Education, Sarah Levine, Sara Lawrence-Lightfoot, Greg Martin, Jonathan Martin, David Perkins, Ron Ritchhart, Susan Rosenholtz, Steve Seidel, Michael Thompson and his co-authors, and Grant Wiggins

- The managers and *listeros* of the ISED-L listserv, who have created a vibrant community of educators, now entering its third decade, who are always there for one another

- Michael Brosnan, who assigned me the *Independent School* magazine article that gave birth to this book.

- Harry Hart, who long ago shared with me Grant Wiggins' "The Futility of Trying to Teach Everything of Importance"—just the bag of new tricks that this old dog needed.

- My colleagues over the years at The Gow School, Providence Country Day, Fessenden School, Beaver Country Day School, the Independent Curriculum Group, and One Schoolhouse, who have given me a world of wisdom; special thanks to Rob Connor, Debi Ellman, Lesley Colognesi, Kader Adjout, Peter Hutton, Nadine Nelson, Rebecca Yacono, Bill Rice, Evan West, Rod Eaton, Brad Rathgeber, and my late uncle Norman W. Howard.

- The participants and my fellow staff members of several years at the New England New Teacher Seminar, where we tried to practice what this book preaches.

- Nancy Raley and the Publications Office at the National Association of Independent Schools—in fact, everyone at NAIS, whose encouragement gave birth to this book and whose willingness to involve me in numerous projects through the years—shout out to Jefferson Burnett!—helped me amass much of the perspective I have tried to share here.

- My late spouse, Mimi Harrington, and our children, Nat and Will, who in their childhoods yielded the living room and then the porch without ever yielding in their love and editorial support as this book was being written (and who are both teachers themselves now!); the work ethic of our Sudanese foster-son, John Bul Kuol, has been an inspiration; and my son Sam's enthusiasm for writing has been an incentive.

- Special friends in the school and writing realm who have shared with me their confidence, strength, and wisdom—especially Tiffany Hendryx, Catherine Conover Covert, Kate Rabinov, and Nat Philbrick.

And finally, I join the legions who are in debt to the wisdom and encouragement of David Mallery. Late in life I found a true mentor.

www.ingramcontent.com/pod-product-compliance
Lightning Source LLC
Chambersburg PA
CBHW032103280326
41933CB00009B/743